About Island Press

Since 1984, the nonprofit organization Island Press has been stimulating, shaping, and communicating ideas that are essential for solving environmental problems worldwide. With more than 1,000 titles in print and some 30 new releases each year, we are the nation's leading publisher on environmental issues. We identify innovative thinkers and emerging trends in the environmental field. We work with world-renowned experts and authors to develop cross-disciplinary solutions to environmental challenges.

Island Press designs and executes educational campaigns, in conjunction with our authors, to communicate their critical messages in print, in person, and online using the latest technologies, innovative programs, and the media. Our goal is to reach targeted audiences—scientists, policy makers, environmental advocates, urban planners, the media, and concerned citizens—with information that can be used to create the framework for long-term ecological health and human well-being.

Island Press gratefully acknowledges major support from The Bobolink Foundation, Caldera Foundation, The Curtis and Edith Munson Foundation, The Forrest C. and Frances H. Lattner Foundation, The JPB Foundation, The Kresge Foundation, The Summit Charitable Foundation, Inc., and many other generous organizations and individuals.

The opinions expressed in this book are those of the author(s) and do not necessarily reflect the views of our supporters.

DIY City

DIY City

THE COLLECTIVE POWER OF SMALL ACTIONS

Hank Dittmar

ISLANDPRESS | Washington | Covelo

Library of Congress Control Number: 2019952651

All Island Press books are printed on
environmentally responsible materials.

Manufactured in the United States of America
10 9 8 7 6 5 4 3 2 1

Keywords: affordable housing, Congress for the New Urbanism, Do It
Yourself, entrepreneurship, green infrastructure, housing, Lean Urbanism,
London, Prince Charles's Foundation for the Built Environment, resilience,
Santa Monica airport, slack, Surface Transportation Policy Project
(STPP), Tactical Urbanism, transportation, Whole Earth Catalog

Contents

Acknowledgments

This book is a testament to what can be accomplished when colleagues and friends from far-flung places work together for a common good. When he died in 2018, my husband, Hank Dittmar, was working against time to complete his final book, *DIY City*, as a distillation of what he had learned about cities and what makes them great over his long career as a planner, manager, and organizer. My family and I are grateful to all the colleagues and friends who have donated countless hours to shepherding the manuscript to publication. It would be impossible to acknowledge everyone who contributed to Hank's original manuscript and all those who, since his death, have contributed anecdotes, illustrations, updates, and friendship. But I am going to try.

We gratefully acknowledge a grant from the Ford Foundation to help underwrite publication, and Don Chen, then at the Ford Foundation and now president of the Surdna Foundation, for his encouragement; Heather Boyer, our editor at Island Press, and the team there that helped us solve a myriad of large and small problems; and colleagues around the world, including Dr. Anthony Perl of Simon Fraser University, Vancouver; Eric Reynolds, founding director of Urban Space Management in London; Judi Barker, owner of the Barker Hangar in Santa Monica, California; Lisa Schamess and many supportive colleagues at the Congress for the New Urbanism;

Robin Rather, a longtime friend and advisor from Austin, Texas; Kevin Kinzinger, formerly a collaborator in the Lean Urbanism pilot in Savannah, Georgia; and Tom Downs, once Hank's boss and always his colleague and friend.

This book could not have happened without the help of friends and colleagues from Hank's tenure with The Prince's Foundation, including Hooper Brooks, who identified key people at the foundation and in the international community who could help us "fill in the blanks" and provided relevant documents; members and former members of the foundation staff who supplied photographs and reports that informed the sections on Rose Town and London, including Joey Tabone, Matthew Hardy, Ben Bolger, and Tim Goodwin; and Richard Ivey, who often served as the foundation's official photographer during Hank's tenure. Longtime colleagues, collaborators, and coauthors Scott Bernstein and Brian Falk made major contributions to the chapters about Washington at war and Lean Urbanism. Old friends of ours from early days in Austin, particularly Richard Linklater and Ric Cruz, contributed to the book and supplied images for the concept of "slack" and for the punk music scene of the early 1980s.

Thanks to Sarah Campbell, an old friend and colleague from Washington, Austin, and London, who worked tirelessly to find illustrations, obtain permissions, and make sure that Hank's legacy was fully encompassed; and to Margaret O'Dell, also a longtime colleague and friend of Hank's, who took files from multiple computers and conversations with multiple sources and massaged them into a final manuscript.

We are grateful to you all.

Kelle Dittmar

Introduction

by Margaret O'Dell

My ideal city is one that marries the best of the past with the best of the future. . . . It's about bringing together the things that we love about the traditional city and connecting them so we can enjoy quality of life. It's not a technology problem—it's a working-together problem.

I believe that people matter, and that we can engage people in planning and sustainability processes in a way that positively affects the outcome.

—*Hank Dittmar*

HANK DITTMAR—urban planner by training, friend of artists and creatives, sometime rancher, "high priest of town planning" to The Prince of Wales—loved cities and their promise for a sustainable future. He foresaw a day when more and more people would be living in cities without sacrificing quality of life, in a built environment that suited its place, and with many opportunities for community connection. But his views were also shaped by his experience at Northwestern University, where in the 1970s the sociologist John McKnight had begun to talk about building on the existing assets in even the poorest community. Like McKnight, Hank saw cities as offering assets to build with, both the human capital of those who lived there and the capital of the existing built environment.

Hank believed in letting small things happen. Remarking on the famous dictum of the urban planner Daniel Burnham, "Make no little plans; they have no magic to stir men's blood," Hank concluded that big plans were often the problem. Looking at the global cities of the world, he saw a crisis of success, with gentrification and global capital looking for a safe haven combining to drive up home prices in some cities while others decayed for lack of investment. These trends affected middle- and working-class residents, who traditionally had found owning their own home to be the safest investment, and young people trying to establish themselves and coping with the vagaries of a gig economy. Hank thought the answers would be found by looking to places and times where, for one reason or another—reduced oversight from regulatory agencies in Detroit, a pressing need to house an expanded workforce in World War II–era Washington, abandoned factories and warehouses in Manhattan and Austin, Texas, where young artists could squat and experiment—the financial and regulatory barriers that hinder individual initiative, small business, and small-scale development were relaxed. Those lessons could be captured and replicated to make the most of cities as places where people can flourish.

Over the course of his career, as the various settings described in the chapters of this book indicate, Hank Dittmar came to see cities as systems with parallels in nature. The healthiest such urban system is not a monoculture of tall buildings built at one time, but a place where, as in a forest, a multitude of small and varied communities flourish in niches, and succession happens gradually over time. Looking over the series of examples offered in these chapters, something else becomes clear: none of them is permanent, but each is in process and each presents something to learn from. And we can say about Hank's ideas and projects what his hero Jane Jacobs said about the books she wrote: "Each one is like a child. You send it out into the world, and you don't know what will happen to it there."

The municipal airport at Santa Monica offers one object lesson. During Hank's five years as the director of the airport, the underused facility took on a new life, providing benefits to a variety of constituencies as well as to the private pilots who had been its primary users. The airport got a new administration building, improved runways, new noise abatement rules in response to the complaints of neighborhood residents, and additional safety improvements. It also acquired two new restaurants, an observation deck where families could watch planes take off and land, a Museum of Flying, and a satellite arts campus of Santa Monica College. Among the "meantime uses" in underused airport buildings were various small businesses, pop-up shops and art exhibits, and glittering events such as the MTV and NBA awards.

Today the Santa Monica Airport is slated to close when its federal agreement runs out in 2028. Parking surrounding the Barker Hangar, a multipurpose facility that is central to the adaptive reuse story of the airport, is already being redeveloped as semiprivate soccer fields, although the hangar itself will continue as an events venue until the airport closes. The single runway is being shortened to discourage private jets, though the Santa Monica Landmark Commission has agreed to preserve an iconic "compass rose," a navigational aid that was painted onto the runway in the days before instrument flying by a group of the nation's first women pilots, including Amelia

Earhart, and restored by the same group in 1985, with Hank's support. A higher-end restaurant has closed, and the popular casual restaurant is still open but squeezed by rising rent and upgrade requirements. Airport buildings that housed a rich variety of small businesses, workshops, and artists' studios were leased for commercial office space and then released to Snap Inc., the parent company of Snapchat. And that transfer offers another lesson in urban succession: in moving to the Santa Monica Airport, Snap is abandoning its original quarters in the somewhat funkier Venice Beach area, where it had been a spur to local development. Officials there are wondering what comes next for their community and hoping that the vacated buildings will attract smaller businesses and start-ups.

The story of doubling up in Washington, DC, during wartime shows how the available housing stock can be used flexibly to accommodate fluctuations in population. Hank was a believer in the contemporary utility of accessory dwelling units, often called "granny flats." He saw making multifamily units possible in areas zoned for single-family occupancy as a way of accommodating the changing demographics of smaller families, empty nesters living in much bigger houses than they need or sometimes can afford, and young singles delaying the home and car ownership that signified adulthood for their parents' generation. But World War II–era Washington made shared housing work through a strategy of changing both public attitudes and restrictive local rules. After the war, housing markets reverted, and suburban development, growth in auto ownership, and public investments in highway building rendered doubling up unnecessary for decades.

Contemporary Washington faces another housing squeeze, and in 2016, Harriet Tregoning, the director of the DC Office of Planning under two mayors and a close ally of Hank's, rewrote the city's zoning rules to permit the construction of accessory dwelling units in neighborhoods zoned for single-family-only residences. That program is being imitated in suburbs such as Montgomery County, which passed similar rules in 2019. Though only 400–500 accessory units have been created so far, throughout the Washington metro area, and in largely single-family-home cities such as Minneapolis and Seattle, adding accessory units and building multifamily housing are both legal and increasingly encouraged by local officials. That said, anecdotes from the Washington, DC, area; Minneapolis; and Austin suggest that (as the Lean Urbanists have noted) changing the rules is only half the battle. A creative person with a small project may still find that decision-makers don't understand the nuances of their own codes or that members of the community fear and oppose changes to residency patterns. Without the added pressure of wartime, changing attitudes may be a slower process than it was in Washington in the 1940s.

Prominent urbanists celebrate the role of "creatives" and argue that a vibrant arts scene makes a city a place where more people want to be. Richard Florida of the University of Toronto, among other scholars, has argued that the arts stimulate economies, and statements from large corporations such as Boeing and McDonald's (when they moved their corporate headquarters to downtown Chicago) confirm that being near arts scenes and centers of higher education make it easier for them to recruit the workers they want.[1,2]

What Hank saw and celebrated was that "slack"—sufficient space and time for creativity to flourish—was not only a key ingredient to a successful twenty-first-century city but also necessary to help society adjust to the changing nature of the economy and of work. The buildings that once held factories could now provide space for start-ups, pop-ups, music studios, and restaurants. People could use the time not committed to the traditional nine-to-five job to learn new skills—teaching themselves to be writers, musicians, and artists—or to learn to do things for themselves without needing to rely on experts. They could start shops or urban farms. (Judi Barker, the owner of the Barker Hangar at the Santa Monica Airport, tells of once putting on a circus, elephants and all, without a permit, and of a store that operated for years at the airport without a fourth wall, since as a temporary structure it faced a much lower bar for permits and inspections.) Public policies that could facilitate this use of both spatial and temporal slack could support new small businesses, encourage small-scale building and renovation, work-from-home, and other low-cost ways of adapting to the new world of work.

Rose Town, Jamaica, is one of these stories with both a happy ending and an object lesson. When two halves of a town divided by a gang war came together to revitalize their community, led by the grandmothers, it was an inspiring moment. But the object lesson, which also threads through all the narratives in these chapters, came when one Rose Town resident asked poignantly, "When is the Prince going to give me my new house?" and it became clear that capacity building had to be the first order of business. Communities, we see with increasing clarity, can be revitalized only by recognizing and drawing on their own strengths. If the solutions are handed down by experts, whether in the form of master plans or charrettes, the community doesn't engage. If they are allowed to DIY (that is, Do It Yourself), as they do in Rose Town, or to test a vision of a better community, as they do in Tactical Urbanism, incremental and resilient city building becomes possible.

Though so-called meanwhile uses aren't expected to be permanent, the experience of Eric Reynolds in reviving underused parts of London suggests that, with the right kind of backing, a meanwhile use can give way to another meanwhile use rather than just banking land until another luxury high-rise can be built. Having seen his very successful development of Spitalfields Market as an arts-and-crafts-driven space with food vendors and public events supplanted by restaurant chains and fast-fashion brands when the Borough of London took over management, Reynolds decided to make his next "meanwhile" development more permanent. His solution was to secure essentially permanent control of the real estate, place it in trust, and dedicate a portion of revenue from the project to subsidizing arts activities on-site. This strategy ensures an affordable venue for creatives and for experimentation, and it could be applied by public or private entities in any place where adaptive reuse of historic buildings for artists and small businesses can support the kind of creative energy that makes cities great. Coincidentally, this kind of support for the small-scale can nourish a DIY creative community and avert disasters such as the Ghost Ship fire (see chapter 7), which can occur when squatters occupy virtually abandoned buildings and little effort is made to make those buildings safely habitable.

By the last phase of Hank's career, these lessons had come together for him in the concept of Lean Urbanism. Lean Urbanism puts small-scale, locally led development into practice by empowering small-scale developers, community enterprise, and DIY builders. Bringing together local officials, regulators, businesspeople, and community members to identify and overcome barriers, Lean Urbanism can make local improvements such as new or renovated housing, commercial spaces, and community assets like rental kitchens and other business incubators. Ideally, this kind of process, focused in a geographic area plagued by neglect and underinvestment and with underutilized human and infrastructure assets, can bring underground economic activity into the light, make communities both more productive and more livable, and improve people's sense of what their neighborhood can be.

Taken together, the examples in this book offer answers for the future of cities in the industrialized world. Both the Great Recession of 2008 and the hyperfueled development that followed have made housing less affordable and cities less livable. All too often, rehabilitation projects in historic cities have begun with an expensive makeover that destroys what's special about the urban fabric and results in a development burdened by outsize capital costs. And too often, overly general zoning and building requirements render the creative use of slack to meet changing housing needs and the adaptive repurposing of existing buildings impossible. People in the middle, young people starting out, and the poor are increasingly left out. And failing to make space for experimentation and the arts makes cities poorer.

In the mixed-use revival of the Santa Monica Airport, as well as Rose Town, the Barker Hangar, the Custard Factory, and other places where residents and tenants were empowered to do their own rehabs, we find an alternative model for urban revival. It involves doing intentionally what these places discovered by accident: Support "meanwhile" uses and maintain the places where they can happen. Encourage urban homesteading, and let residents design their own cohabiting communities.

Make housing supply more elastic by facilitating doubling up. Forget the real estate planning dogma of "highest and best use," and let development occur incrementally and on a small scale. Combine an incremental approach with a long-term strategy to ensure that small, Main Street–type businesses, maker spaces, and mixed uses won't be squeezed out by successive waves of big projects. Keep the best of what's old and build on it to make cities into places where people can flourish.

Chapter 1

Cities Are Back

ONE OF THE STRANGEST CONTROVERSIES in America in the Clinton years was the furor over "Midnight Basketball." This innocuous community-based initiative aimed to give inner-city youth something to do in the evenings in order to keep them away from gang life and off the streets. Yet it became a symbol for Democrats' coddling of urban youth, and it perfectly expressed the distaste and fear of cities that characterized the American national discourse up through the mid-1990s. Similar dystopian imaginings ruled in Great Britain during the Thatcher years, with fears about so-called sink estates (public housing with high rates of poverty) and the decline of once-powerful manufacturing centers.

Within a decade, however, Americans elected a community organizer from Chicago as president, and within two decades pundits were decrying gentrification and rising home prices in inner cities in the United States and Canada, Europe, and Australia.

Here and now, in what is already being called the Century of the City, it seems mighty strange that during the eight years of his presidency (1993–2001), William Jefferson

Clinton never used the words *city* or *urban* in his speeches or other public utterances. The stock of cities had sunk so low that Clinton's message mavens decreed that he could mention communities or neighborhoods but not the cities of which they were a part. Urban places prompted mental images of crime, riots, and menacing people of color.

This public relations dictum was a legacy of decades of city shaming, from the race riots of the sixties through the well-chronicled garbage strikes and bankruptcies of New York City, and of public policy favoring the growing suburbs. Cities were characterized as dangerous places and were thought to be in terminal decline, and politicians of both parties competed for the suburban vote.

As a city lover, I hated all the demonizing. To me, cities were lively cultural centers and places of diversity and promise. I had begun my career as an outreach worker with street-gang kids in Chicago's inner city and had lived in Los Angeles and San Francisco. During Bill Clinton's presidency, I was leading a nonprofit coalition in Washington, DC, focused on urban transportation policy. True, when I moved to DC, it was led by a crack-addicted night owl of a mayor, and the drinking water was intermittently polluted with *E. coli* bacteria, but the townhouses of Capitol Hill and the apartments of DuPont Circle and Kalorama offered a quality of life that couldn't be beat.

Among the public policies that fueled the suburban explosion in postwar America were low-interest Veterans' Administration loans enabling returning servicemen to buy homes, the mortgage interest tax deduction favoring home ownership, and the building of interstate highways that offered quick access to these new bedroom communities. These subsidies all primed the pump for suburbia and prompted the middle-class

flight and tax drain that left the inner cities increasingly seg-
regated and poor.

I would like to think that our campaigns against sprawl
and for better urban transport, improved public housing, and
city living in mixed-use neighborhoods were the determining
factor in a profound urban rebirth. It would be nice to believe
that research and activism helped to reverse the anti-urban
prejudice that had infected the home-buying public, the media,
and national politicians.

Actually, though, I suspect that it was television and films
that turned the tide, by depicting city living as alluring and
attractive to my generation of young adults. Yes, I put the urban
revival down to TV series like *Seinfeld*, *Sex and the City*, and
Friends and to films like *Bridget Jones's Diary*.

Hollywood had produced decades of films like *Panic in Nee-
dle Park*, *Taxi Driver*, and *Escape from New York* that painted a
dystopian vision of urban conditions, alongside long-running
series such as *My Three Sons*, *The Brady Bunch*, and *Family Ties*
that idealized life in leafy white suburbs.

Seinfeld and *Friends* changed all that, depicting smart,
quippy, and good-looking young singles who lived in apartments and hung out in diners, cafés, and bars. They were having
fun, doing interesting work, and seemed to live in a milieu filled
entirely with other attractive, friendly young adults. A generation growing up in the suburbs saw this picture and responded.

The lifestyle of these urban sitcoms was a sanitized version
of what my generation had experienced moving to inner-city
Manhattan, London, San Francisco, or Los Angeles in the
seventies and eighties. City living offered excitement, music,
art, and above all, cheap rent. People inhabited disused warehouses, storefronts, walk-up apartments, and residential hotels.

Perhaps we were "slumming," but it turns out that we were taking the time to explore just what we wanted to be and using what seemed to be the open terrain of the city to do so.

The people who wrote those sitcoms and films, acted in them, and composed the soundtracks lived in warehouses and walk-ups and worked at Second City or the Actor's Studio or scrabbled around LA trying to sell a script. When it came time to write the story, they wrote the story of their city life, cleaned up and romanticized for TV.

The effect began to be noticeable in the nineties, as young bankers, lawyers, and media types started pricing out both working-class people and artists for flats in Manhattan, San Francisco, and London's Islington. Favorite restaurants began to fill up, and new ones opened as steak-and-sushi joints, and concept restaurants with ambitious chefs moved in. Storefronts once occupied by makeshift galleries or flats got remade into upscale chain retail. And former shot-and-beer bars and working people's pubs began to feature designer cocktails.

The twenty-somethings were followed by middle-class hipsters sniffing out where to invest. The government took note as well, seeking to prop up the newly fashionable creative economy with cultural institutions and support for tech businesses.

Cities were cool, and certain cities were especially cool; cities with downtown cred, universities, and cultural institutions all seemed to launch first in the urban revival. It turned out that the presence of both mainstream arts culture and a productive arts environment was as important to city vitality as bridges, tunnels, and subway systems.

Close-in urban neighborhoods once thought too gritty became desirable, and the old four-step gentrification process—risk-oblivious artists and gays, followed by risk-aware young people, then by risk-averse dentists investing in property, and finally by big developers and chain stores—became a two-step process, with government-backed regeneration companies and investors paving the way for the big property developers.

So the thing city lovers had long been waiting for finally happened, and urban districts were on the upswing, initially in world-facing metropolises including London, New York, the San Francisco Bay Area, Singapore, Vancouver, Toronto, Melbourne, and Berlin. Real estate companies began to tout investing in the twenty-four-hour city. Posh magazines began to publish city livability indexes, and cities began to compete to get on them.

Urban rock stars emerged to guide city leaders in becoming cool. Urban theorist Richard Florida promoted the "creative economy," a concept based on academic research showing that cities with clusters of so-called cultural creatives—media, architects, and professionals like accountants and bankers—were outperforming cities without such agglomerations. Jan Gehl got famous reminding everyone of what used to be common sense: that streets were for people, not cars. Various South American mayors developed lucrative speaking careers and obtained Harvard posts based on building busways and pedestrianizing city precincts.

When centuries of soot were scraped off St. Paul's Cathedral, Sir Christopher Wren's masterpiece in London, it seemed a metaphor for the bright and shiny future that was in store for historic cities worldwide as the century turned. City-center populations were growing in big and even medium-sized cities in the developed world. City economies were booming in these so-called creative cities, which were magnets for young people, tech industry, and finance and media. Crime was way down.

Cities that had been seen as dangerous, dirty, and polluting were now considered vibrant, lively, and sustainable. Research began to show that urban residents contribute fewer pollutants on a per capita basis than suburbanites, as they drive less, occupy less space, and are more likely to live in multifamily dwellings. Business responded, with many of the new tech giants choosing to locate in urban centers. Facebook and Google notably shunned the suburban corporate campuses favored by companies in the late twentieth century. Many Fortune 500 companies that had built such campuses have chosen to relocate to downtowns. In recent years, McDonald's, Motorola, General Electric, Aetna, and Marriott International all have abandoned the suburbs for city centers in Chicago, Boston, and Manhattan.

These trends combined with an explosion of mobile investment capital across the world, generated by an emergent Asian middle class and by the concentration of wealth in the Middle East, in former Soviet Bloc countries, and in booming Asian countries. After the major recession that began in 2007, it seemed that property investment in "hot" cities in stable countries like Britain, the United States, Canada, and Australia was the best way to secure one's capital and generate double-digit returns.

The glass-sheathed residential tower—a property type developed in Singapore—soon began to pop up in all of the popular cities: Melbourne and Sydney in Australia, Vancouver and Toronto in Canada, London, and New York. Funded by offshore companies and marketed overseas, these luxury towers became ubiquitous. According to the *Guardian*, 40 percent of all new-build properties in 2016 in the London Borough of Westminster went to foreign buyers, and all of the apartments in the Heygate development in South London went to foreign buyers.

In Canada, Vancouver and Toronto have been particular targets for foreign buyers, with many luxury properties marketed solely in Asia. Data from Vancouver shows that 40 percent of the high-end market was owned by offshore investors prior to the imposition of a recent "empty homes" tax on non-resident owners.[1] (The Province of British Columbia has also instituted a tax on speculative investment; both taxes aim to raise revenue to support the development of affordable housing while encouraging absentee owners to rent out their properties.) This point was driven home to me one evening in 2008 when I dined at the Vancouver home of my colleague and collaborator Dr. Anthony Perl. Anthony lives in a so-called point tower (a tall, slender building with floors built around a central elevator core and minimal hallways) on the Vancouver waterfront. When I arrived I noticed how quiet his neighborhood was, even in the early evening. Anthony confirmed that he was one of only a few people resident in his tower and that most units were bought and sold as investments without ever being occupied.

As I walked back to my hotel through a dense district of tall buildings, I reflected on how similar the eerie quiet was to that I experienced when I visited my friend Dominic Richards just off Sloane Square in London, another district largely in the hands of wealthy absentee owners as second and third homes.[2] This pattern of ownership is being repeated in big cities around the world, with predictable consequences for city neighborhoods. In addition to the affordable-housing crunch created if much of the available housing stock is owned by people who never occupy it, crime or at least neighborhood decay hurts the entire community. A group of citizens in Vancouver created a blog called Beautiful Empty Homes to call attention to neighborhoods where older people who were surrounded by unoccupied houses felt unsafe and to such extreme examples as a million-dollar house that had become home to a den of coyotes.[3]

Residential towers along the Vancouver, BC, waterfront.
(Credit: photo by Christopher Woo.)

Throughout most of history, housing was shelter, and even for those who made their livings as builders and developers, the aim was to produce a steady income from rents. Even pension funds held property to derive predictable income from rents, not from uplift in value. In fact, value remained mostly static.

In the past thirty years, though, property has been transformed and commodified into a number of well-defined investment vehicles. For most Britons and most North Americans, their biggest investment is in their home—more than their savings or retirement accounts. In big, successful cities, property and land have become the place for international investors to stash cash, in hopes of a quick and significant return and also because real estate is seen as a safe harbor.

This has led to two major crises: unaffordable housing and increased inequality. At the same time, this conversion of property into investment undermines cities as successful places to live, work, and create. The impact is especially severe for young adults, the so-called millennial generation. A report by the United Kingdom's Resolution Foundation found

> the generation currently aged 18–36 are typically spending over a third of their post-tax income on rent or about 12 percent on mortgages, compared with 5–10 percent of income spent by their grandparents in the 1960s and 1970s. Despite spending more, young people today are more likely to live in overcrowded and smaller spaces, and face longer journeys to work—commuting for the equivalent of three days a year more than their parents.[4]

In 1996, it took 3.6 times the annual wage to buy a home in the UK; in mid-2019, it takes 6 times annual earnings and 8 times annual wages in London. The picture is equally dire when it comes to renting, with average renters in London spending up to 61 percent of their income on rent, depending on neighborhood. Of course, as we enter 2020 and Britain awaits the resolution of Brexit, there is some fluctuation in these numbers, but the overall change in affordability over two decades still excludes those not in the highest-earning categories from urban life.

The affordability crunch hits "hot" metro areas in the United States just as hard. According to the Paragon Real Estate Group, just 21 percent of San Francisco Bay Area households could afford to buy a house at the median sales price in 2017, and in the city and county of San Francisco, just 12 percent could afford the median-priced home.

As home prices increase, the impact is felt severely by minority households, who can find themselves priced out of the market altogether, according to US real estate research company Redfin. In 2016, just 18 percent of homes in the thirty largest metro areas were affordable for those earning the median income for Hispanic households, and 14 percent were affordable for families earning the median income for African American households. Both rates were down 11 percentage points from 2012. This is compared to 30 percent affordable for those earning the median income for white households, down 12 percentage points since 2012. Lack of affordability in Denver, Los Angeles, Portland, San Francisco, San Diego, and Phoenix is especially severe. In each of these markets, fewer than 5 percent of homes for sale are affordable for those at the median income level for African American and Hispanic families.

One study asked whether growing inequality and wealth concentration in a city could lead to higher house prices. Economists Janna Matlack and Jacob Vigdor concluded that this seemed to be so in metropolitan areas with tight housing markets "where incomes are rising rapidly at the high end of the distribution, while incomes at the low end trend upward only slowly if at all. In housing markets with greater slack, or where increased inequality reflects declines at the low end more than increases at the high end, the impact of inequality appears more benign."[5] In other words, an influx of people at the higher end, when coupled with a tight housing market, can drive up prices and thus increase disparity by forcing those on fixed or lower incomes to devote a larger share of their income to shelter.

Cities are now recognized as the engines of both local and global economies. Driven by a rediscovery of city living by the young, and by the shift away from resource extraction to service- and finance-driven economies, a group of big cities in the developed world have become global magnets for both talent and capital. As capital floods in, prices go up, and developers tend to build both for investors and for the wealthy. As a result, supply tightens for rental, entry-level, and mid-level properties, driving these prices up.

This shift toward urban living thus carries within it the seeds of its own demise. The conditions that made some cities places of innovation and creativity are threatened by the very success of those cities. Affordable housing, educational and cultural institutions, and a thriving artistic and social scene for the young are all necessary parts of the city mix, and the influx of globally mobile capital into urban real estate drives up land values, property prices, and rents, creating difficult if not impossible conditions for all but the wealthy.

Government alone can't ensure that creative cities thrive and are sustained, or that opportunity is available to a broad spectrum of young adults to enter into and thrive in our successful cities. However well intentioned, government tends to homogenize when it comes to urban revival, to favor big players rather than small, and to fall into the trap of creating capital value rather than social capital.

While big utopian plans get a lot of attention, most great cities and towns are the product of many hands working over many generations, and they are the better for it. London, one of the world's most treasured and successful cities, represents the knitting together of many villages and numerous speculative developments dating back to the eighteenth century. And apart from land being platted into grids, most prewar American cities and towns grew as the result of individual businesspeople and local companies making one building or one street at a time.

In recent years, in the face of some worrying global trends, impending crises including global climate change, and massive migration of refugees fleeing natural disasters and failed states, the notion of sustainability has been complemented by the idea of resiliency, or the ability of our society and especially our built environment to withstand shock and bounce back. Large amounts of philanthropic capital are being poured into creating resilient cities and resilient systems, much of it focused on either construction of new buildings and infrastructure or "smart city" data, monitoring, and performance systems.

Resilience is an important idea, and it is a concept that seems to have rapidly overtaken *sustainability* in the buzzword Olympics. Judith Rodin, former president of the Rockefeller Foundation and author of *The Resilience Dividend*, put it this way: "Resilience is the ability of people, communities, and institutions to prepare for, withstand, and bounce back more rapidly from acute shocks and chronic stresses."[6] During Rodin's term at the Rockefeller Foundation, the foundation invested heavily in promoting resilience, founding the 100 Resilient Cities Challenge, which funded cities to appoint Chief Resilience Officers and develop resilience plans, and promoting learning exchanges among city officials, environmentalists, and nonprofit leaders. While the foundation has since gone in a different direction, resilience initiatives at the national and local level are continuing the projects initiated with that funding and sharing information about how cities can become more resilient.

Approaches being pioneered by these cities include new technology, financial instruments, resilience indexes, and systems for data collection and performance monitoring. Many cities are looking at infrastructure for flood resilience in response to both impending sea-level rise and the increased rate of river and surface flooding in cities and towns due to extreme storm events. And people are looking at greening their cities with buildings covered in plants and topped by orchards, all sustained by complex trellis and irrigation systems.

In addition to looking forward at new building, new construction, and new technology, one might also look back at the ways that cities have adapted over time, uncovering some important lessons about the resilience of the traditional city and the resilience of traditional culture. The futurist Stewart Brand, founding editor of the *Whole Earth Catalog*, has developed a theory of how change occurs in the world, from the rapid changes of fashion through increasingly slower paces of change for infrastructure, governance, and—slowest of all—nature. Smaller changes increase the opportunity for adaptation and resilience.

Traditional cities evolve from both the bottom up and the top down in terms of initiative and energy. More and more what we need is for top-down planning and thinking and governance to recognize and allow for the contribution of bottom-up entrepreneurship and community-building.

Green infrastructure to manage stormwater in Hinsdale, Illinois. (Credit: Center for Neighborhood Technology, 2014.)

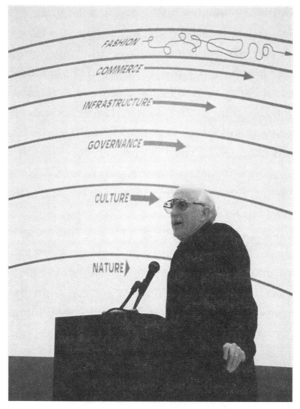

Stewart Brand presents his theory of pace layers of
change in 2003. (Credit: original resolution photo by
curiouslee is licensed under CC BY 2.0.)

Government policy can, however, create the conditions
for smaller-scale initiatives to flourish, the space for "scenes"
to happen, and the circumstances that allow people without
money but with ideas to explore those ideas, whether they are
messing with technology, with music, or with craft.

Chapter 2

Sometimes the Small Stuff Sticks: Learning to Improvise

AT AGE TWENTY-EIGHT I became the director of the Santa Monica Airport, a busy general aviation airport surrounded by homes and in striking distance of wealthy enclaves including Malibu, Beverly Hills, and Pacific Palisades. Appointed during a takeover of this formerly sleepy beach city by the Santa Monicans for Renters' Rights, I was asked to implement an uneasy truce between neighbors who wanted to close the airport and an aviation community that brandished a federal agreement stipulating that the airport must remain open in perpetuity. The compromise agreement set forth an ambitious plan to both improve the airport and enhance the surrounding community. What I learned during my six-year tenure at the airport reshaped my thinking about cities and human nature.

As a planner and urban designer, I was trained to make plans—the bigger the better. And the received history of city and town planning is filled with great plans, from Sir Thomas More's Utopia up through Baron Haussmann's remake of medieval Paris into today's grand boulevards and Pierre L'Enfant's Washington, DC. The "City Beautiful" plans of Daniel Burnham, Frederick Law Olmsted, and John Nolen all left an indelible imprint on America's cities. Burnham famously said, "Make no little plans; they have no magic to stir men's blood."

At architecture and planning school I was exposed to these and more modern idealists, including French modernist Le Corbusier, whose Ville Radieuse proposed to destroy central Paris and abolish the "tyranny of the street," and Frank Lloyd Wright, whose Broadacre City was an even more spread-out version of the already sprawling American suburb.

Yet even as I learned about large-scale regional planning and the design of new settlements, I was drawn to the work of Christopher Alexander, whose 1977 book on livable urban design, *A Pattern Language*, described an artisanal, organic approach to city planning. I also fell in love with the work of Jane Jacobs, who wrote about the walkable, mixed-use city from close observation rather than theory. In fact, my master's thesis contrasted Alexander's approach to cities with the utopian ideas of Le Corbusier's Ville Radieuse and Frank Lloyd Wright's Broadacre City and tried to identify a way of putting Alexander's patterns into practice through community participation.

Early in my career, I got to make some big plans myself. As noted above, as a progressive planner in my twenties, I became the People's Republic of Santa Monica's airport director. Santa Monica had recently been transformed from a sleepy, working-class town into a hotbed of community activism and renters' rights by Santa Monicans for Renters' Rights and the Campaign for Economic Democracy. Former Students for a

Democratic Society leader Tom Hayden represented us in the state senate, making his wife Jane Fonda—dubbed Hanoi Jane by the press for her visit to North Vietnam at the height of the war there—our First Lady. SMRR, as the Renters' Rights crowd was known, was part of a localist counterpoint to the Reagan Revolution in towns like Burlington, Cleveland, Madison, Ann Arbor, Boulder, Austin, Berkeley, and Santa Cruz.

As airport director, I was expected to implement a just-ratified 1984 Airport Agreement between the City of Santa Monica, proprietor of the Santa Monica Airport, and the Federal Aviation Administration. The agreement resolved litigation between the City and the entire aviation community, resulting from the City's intention to close the airport due to both concerns over noise and the desire to build housing. Unfortunately for that plan, the City had promised the federal government to keep the airport open in perpetuity when it took the airport back at the end of the Second World War.

The airport agreement, which committed the City to redevelop and improve aviation facilities while capping the number of based aircraft, allowed the city to develop 43 acres of prime West LA real estate for non-airport uses; the agreement also added land to a park and called for a unique, performance-based noise program. At twenty-eight years old, with a few years' planning experience but no aviation experience apart from having grown up around air bases with my Air Force officer father, I was asked to serve as acting airport director. It was a young crowd: City Manager John Alshuler was in his thirties, as were City Attorney Bob Myers, Deputy City Manager Lynne Barrett, and Community and Economic Development Director Mark Tigan. I reported to an ebullient planner named John Jalili, who was the assistant city manager.

Most airport directors had an aviation or military background, and I was not exactly welcomed by the pilots and businesses at the airport, who had learned to mistrust the City. One member of the Santa Monica Airport Association told me at our first meeting that there were three strikes against me. The consensus, though, seemed to be two strikes.

My job was to implement the new airport agreement by moving aviation businesses across to the north side of the runway under new leases, repairing the airport infrastructure, building new hangars and a new terminal and administration building, and putting noise-monitoring equipment off the ends of the runway in order to record and manage the noise made by pilots of individual aircraft. On the runway was painted an old navigational aid, a "compass rose," that was placed there in 1929 by a group of pioneering women pilots, and there was community interest in preserving it.

Over a five-year period, all that got done: new leases and shiny new airport buildings; an aviation museum; a high-end restaurant filled with West Coast art overlooking the runway, and a more midrange one, too; new lighting, taxiways, and hangars; a noise program that banned certain old jets for their performance and taught other aircraft to fly more quietly, reducing overall impact on the community. We also installed a new park next to the airport, began a public art program, and developed interim uses while the City's development officials were beginning a bid process for development of the 43-acre office park. These included a design campus for nearby Santa Monica College and also permitting the use of an old World War II hangar called the Barker Hangar for public events and what today would be called start-ups, maker spaces, and creative industries.

Barker Hangar as an aviation facility. (Credit: provided by Judi Barker.)

The transformation of the Barker Hangar from a big old building storing lots of airplanes into a hotbed for small start-up businesses and a sought-after events venue is a case in point. When I came to the airport, the hangar was managed and owned by James Barker, and it hosted a flight school and a propeller repair shop and provided takedown and storage for a number of general aviation aircraft. Barker was a friendly man whose tenants all cared for him, and his Christmas party was the first one I was invited to at the airport. After his death in 1986, his daughter, Judi Barker, took over management of the hangar. We were of a generation and a mind-set, enjoying the airport scene as well as gigs at the Whisky a Go Go, and she came to me early on for advice. The hangar was on a parcel of land that was then slated to be removed from aviation use, and city economic development staff were formulating plans for a 43-acre, 1.5-million-square-foot business park, very much in an eighties mode of thinking.

Judi and I have kept in touch over the years, and I asked her how she came to move from a purely aviation tenancy to a mix of businesses. She replied,

> When I came to you that day in July of 1986, you told me to stick around as long as I could, but I would need to figure out what to do, as aviation would be leaving the south side of the airport. You suggested incubator businesses. Sure enough, slowly but surely all of the aviation business began to move. The spaces on the side of the hangar were large, but there was not a lot of parking. . . . So the best people to rent to were artists who needed a large room and had one car and were creative enough to blend with the pilots. They all started painting the sky and the airplanes.

The hangar is a huge, clear span building with a central space of 35,000 square feet and a ceiling height of forty-five feet at its apex, and over time, Judi began to promote it for events of up to 2,000 people. It became famous among fashionistas for hosting the Barney's sale, and for a number of years, it served as the venue for the Billboard Music Awards. This posed some challenges, for it was a hangar, not an auditorium, and fire and building officials had trouble finding the correct boxes to tick. Judi remembered,

> In the beginning, when I decided to do events I was closed down by Fire Chief Stein. When he realized I wanted to do things right, and I was not afraid to get down and dirty and do it myself, he helped. From that point on, I kept my word and he kept his, and we've had hardly any problems since. The building department is still clueless. I am the only event/stage in the city now, and their laws cannot apply to me, so no matter what I do, each inspector has his own interpretation of the law, and it is a moving target.

Barker Hangar as a multiuse and events space hosting the MTV Awards. (Credit: provided by Judi Barker, 2018.)

Like many of the heroes in this book, Judi decided what she wanted to do and began to do it, without necessarily asking for permission first. If entrepreneurs do a competent job, often the public officials will recognize that and work cooperatively with them. That certainly was Judi's experience with both the airport director and the fire chief.

Another characteristic of the successful improviser is the belief in doing it with one's own resources. Judi found tenants who could work together as a community. She says,

I had to make a decision as to what businesses would work in a manufacturing area and what I needed to make things work. I learned fast that I had no money to work with. So I rented to a painter, electrician, plumber, fabricator, mechanic, photographer, etc., and we bartered. That is the only way I kept the hangar together. The hangar needed so many repairs that if I had to pay retail I would never have survived. We were all trying to survive, so it was a common thread. If we all kept the hangar together, I could continue to fight and they would continue to have a space for their business. I had thought of turning every-thing into storage, but it takes a village and I wanted to be in a village. I have children of tenants renting from me now—and a grandchild, editor of an art magazine she started.

The noise program worked well, bringing the noise contours entirely within the bounds of the airport. The Barker Hangar, the postmodern-art-filled DC3 restaurant, the rooftop Typhoon café, and Santa Monica College all integrated airport users and the community and began to foster an appreciation for the airport among its neighbors. Perhaps the most success-ful innovation was a simple observation deck overlooking the runway, where a loudspeaker broadcast the communications between pilots and the control tower. It was packed with fami-lies on weekends and after school. By the time I left in 1990, it was clear that the ad hoc activities were a big plus for the airport.

The aviation master plan was implemented successfully as well, with new airport businesses, and this enabled the city to proceed with a procurement effort for developers of the forty-three-acre parcel. An international group of bidders emerged, with famous architects including Kohn Pedersen Fox and Frank Gehry. Huge opposition from neighbors also emerged, as vociferous as the opposition to the airport itself had been—or more so. Concerns were expressed over noise, traffic, and intrusion into neighborhoods. Ultimately, the pro-posal was defeated in a referendum, and the idea of developing the forty-three acres had to be abandoned. The interim uses, including the community that Judi had created at the Barker Hangar, stayed and prospered.

The 1993 federal tax act ushered in a new provision for fractional ownership of jets that led to a boom in corporate flying. The new aviation businesses at the airport began aggressively marketing to visiting jets, and jet traffic boomed. At the same time, the airport directors who followed me determined that the individual counseling and monitoring involved in the performance-based noise program was too onerous, so they abandoned it.

Over the years, both phenomena led to an increase in noise and a resurgence of local opposition to the airport. By the time the airport agreement expired in 2015, the City was trying again to close the airport and enacting measures to restrict its use and harass airport businesses. A new agreement allows them to close the airport down in 2026, the date when the last grant agreement with the Federal Aviation Administration expires. Neighbors hope to replace the airport with a park and a huge expanse of soccer fields, eliminating one of the last bastions of funky small creative business and uniqueness in Santa Monica.

What worked at the airport were the small scale and ad hoc things: moving Santa Monica College design facilities into old airport buildings, which allowed for artist and maker spaces alongside aviation uses, not separate from them; holding events like the Billboard Music Awards in the Barker Hangar; installing the observation deck for children and families; and supporting a range of restaurants. Working with individual pilots also helped, as it personalized the city's concern about noise by challenging them to fly more quietly in keeping with the performance of their aircraft.

The big ideas were less successful and more prey to larger economic trends, with a clearer and more controversial impact and thus greater opposition. They also required substantial capital, which led to continued upward pressure from both the airport businesses in new facilities and the developers. These pressures to expand in turn stimulated more opposition, leading the City to again seek to close the airport when the airport agreement expired in 2015. Of course, I only recognized this cycle over time, as the consequences became clear.

In 1990, I embarked on a new project for the San Francisco Bay Area's Metropolitan Transportation Commission. My job was to manage a project to determine whether to build a new bridge across the San Francisco Bay. Dubbed the Southern Crossing, the new bridge would be located between the Bay Bridge and the San Mateo Hayward Bridge, and had been the subject of long debate. Just after the Loma Prieta earthquake of 1989, the notion of the bridge was pushed by a coalition of engineering and business interests led by State Senator Quentin Kopp, who passed a bill requiring my new employer to study the idea as a first step toward building it. It was an exciting project, and I hurled myself into a study of new bridges around the world, the available technology, and the transportation needs for the facility. We retained a top-notch engineering and transportation planning firm, assembled a steering committee with members ranging from the Sierra Club to the Bay Area Council, the region's business group, and embarked on an intensive program of analysis.

Over the months of study, I became appalled at the multibillion-dollar cost of a new bridge. Our studies showed that while it might relieve congestion on the existing bridges themselves, the new bridge would do little to resolve congestion on the region's overcrowded highways. I was also disturbed to find it would serve cars and enable further sprawl rather than encourage public transit use and more-compact development. Furthermore, the billions required for the bridge would divert funding from other improvements to the transport system. As we presented these results, the initial excitement about the bridge began to fade. Instead we recommended a more incremental approach: improvements to buses, a reconfiguration of subway tunnels in downtown Oakland that would dramatically increase throughput on the BART subway system across the Bay, and an expanded ferry system connecting parts of the region like Alameda and Vallejo to San Francisco. Thirty years later, the bridge is still not built, and by and large, the lack of it is a good thing. But I still didn't realize I had rejected the big plan in favor of the small.

After the study concluded and its recommendations were adopted, I took a position in legislation and finance at the agency and managed their efforts in the state and federal legislature. This included a failed effort at introducing congestion pricing, years before it was implemented in London. I then became involved in the passage of the federal authorization for highway and transit funding. We joined an emerging coalition of groups interested in planning, heritage, public transport and rail, scenic issues, and walking and cycling called the Surface Transportation Policy Project (STPP). The coalition was led by a progressive and pragmatic Texan named Sarah Campbell, one in my personal pantheon of engaged Texas women along with Barbara Jordan, Shirley Chisholm, Ann Richards, Robin Rather, and Molly Ivins. Sarah and her colleagues enlisted the help of Senators Daniel Patrick Moynihan and John Chafee, and the California contingent brought in San Jose congressman Norman Mineta. Together we mounted a sneak attack on the highway lobby and enacted a bill called ISTEA (pronounced "Ice-TEA") that reversed transport policy from the highway-building era back to the community-building era. The bill allowed metropolitan areas to undertake transportation planning, allowed the transfer of funds from highways to transit, put in place funding to tackle air-quality problems, and allocated a specific pot of money for historic facilities such as train stations and for walking, cycling, and hiking, and other creative transportation alternatives, called transportation enhancements. Needing some kind of domestic victory in the aftermath of the first Gulf War, President George H. W. Bush signed the bill on a blustery day in Dallas.

About eighteen months later, in the face of growing opposition from the highway lobby (state highway departments, road-building companies), I moved to Washington, DC, to take up the reins at the STPP coalition, both to ensure that the law was properly implemented and to prepare for its reauthorization. The legislation was an ambitious effort to shift power from the states to metropolitan areas, to move on from a capacity-building era to one of managing the performance of the system, to replace a highways-first policy with a balanced system that recognized that public transit, walking, and cycling were also ways to travel, and to show that environmental and quality of life issues matter.

I stayed in Washington for six years to defend the new law from attack and to try to see that the spirit and the letter of it were fully implemented. Moving from an inside game to a grassroots strategy, we tried to link emergent groups fighting sprawl with advocates for walking, cycling, and rail trails, with preservationists and Main Street businesses, and with down-town business groups and environmental justice advocates. That made for some juicy conversations when we all tried to talk together, but the group worked successfully to provide local releases of reports on pedestrian safety, evaluations of spending under the new law, and other issues. It helped that there was now federal funding available. The local groups soon learned how to advocate for programming those funds to build the local rail trail, rehab the historic train station, or deal with pedestrian-safety issues in poor communities. Over time, members of Congress also learned that one could cut more ribbons for multiple small projects that enhanced communities than for highway projects that cost tens of millions of dollars.

From a twenty-year perspective, the much-hoped-for shift to metropolitan plans only worked in a few places, where regional governments had the muscle to combat the state highway department and the road lobby. The opportunity to "flex" highway funds to public transit was successful in more places, but these were generally in cities and states with well-established public transport. The biggest success was the transportation enhancements program, which funded infrastructure for biking and walking and for historic revitalization. According to the League of American Bicyclists, its funding for many small, locally driven projects scaled up impressively: "In the more than 20 years since the creation of programmatic funding for people who bike and walk more than 22,000 projects have been built and $7.2 billion has been invested in communities."[1] Enhancements funding built a constituency for biking, walking, and historic revitalization all over the country, and this has only grown over the years.

After six years, I left STPP to head a new nonprofit called the Great American Station Foundation, set up by former Amtrak president Tom Downs to improve station facilities as a way to both build Amtrak ridership and revitalize small- and medium-sized towns and cities. The Station Foundation was all about unlocking the power of train station improvement projects to serve as catalysts for city and town revival, particularly in smaller cities and towns. Our chair—Meridian, Mississippi, mayor John Robert Smith—had used transportation enhancement funds to rebuild the Amtrak station in his small city as a community hub, not only for the two trains a day that passed through, but also for bus service and events. It became the most popular place in town for weddings and family reunions, serving both the white and African American communities as perhaps no other local building could, as it was one of the few buildings that had served both communities throughout the history of the small city. We funded similar projects across the country, discovering that rail stations were often the most significant public architecture in these smaller cities and towns. As such, they held a prominent place in the stories and family histories of residents, particularly as people from all classes and walks of life passed through them. Small projects they may have been, but they were powerful symbols of belief in community life. This was evidenced by the coalitions and community groups that came to us for seed grants to do their station plans and designs.

Assuming a new post as chief executive of Prince Charles's Foundation for the Built Environment in 2005, I got to work both at urban design for new communities and with informal settlements in the developing world such as Trench Town in Jamaica, Port au Prince in Haiti, and Libreville in Sierra Leone. I became more and more interested in what we called "urbanization from the bottom up," and its capacity to tap into the inherent resilience of both human and built capital in our cities and towns. In Jamaica, where we became involved after a visit by HRH The Prince of Wales to Trench Town, the objective was to regenerate an inner-city community called Rose Town, a distinct portion of Trench Town off of Spanish Town Road. Prince Charles met a local resident named Michael Black, who had begun to pull the community together. Rose Town had been hard hit by the epidemic of gang and political violence that had plagued Jamaica since the seventies, with Upper Town in the hands of one gang and Lower Town controlled by another. The violence got so bad that the government bulldozed the community's center and allowed it to grow back as bush to keep the two sides apart.

Michael Black resolved to do something about that. He began by gathering the pastors and some of the community's women from both sides of Rose Town for a walk from Upper Town across the no-man's-land in the middle to Lower Town. That led to the formation of the Rose Town Benevolent Society, which was to become our partner in the community.

My predecessor at The Prince's Foundation had made an arrangement with a regeneration company located in Kingston's downtown that was championed by some of the most influential Jamaican families. They had gotten the funding allocated to their company and were holding meetings with the Benevolent Society, and had moved a trailer into Rose Town, filling it with used computers and teaching computer courses. Our donor visited and came back concerned at the lack of action: "They begin and end their meetings with a prayer but do nothing in between."

When I pressed for details of their plan for Rose Town, they told me of a consortium of eminent Jamaican architects and engineers and finally sent through some pictures of new garden apartments for sale to be built on parcels of government land at the fringe of the community. This kind of market-oriented housing was not what Prince Charles had in mind, or what the residents expected, so I put in place a new planning process, led by Andrés Duany of the Miami-based firm of Duany Plater-Zyberk, along with Jamaican architect Ann Hodges. This week-long exercise in community engagement and planning revealed a number of things: the houses in Rose Town were generally well constructed and could be repaired; the residents wished to remain on their parcels, many of which they had occupied when the original inhabitants left during the troubles; and there was desire for job training and the creation of local businesses operated by residents. At the same time, there was a culture of dependency. When I first visited, the most frequent question was, "When will the Prince give me my new house?"

It became clear to me and my colleagues at the foundation that the challenge was first one of social development and only then one of physical improvement, and that master planning had raised expectations of outside intervention when local capacity building was needed. So we used some of our limited funds to hire a social worker named Angela Stultz to work alongside the Benevolent Society in a new nonprofit called the Rose Town Foundation for the Built Environment. Its goal was to enable the Benevolent Society and the residents to make and implant their own plans. Supported by two energetic and brilliant Americans, then US ambassador Brenda Johnson and Montego Bay entrepreneur Michele Rollins, along with Hooper Brooks of my staff, the Rose Town Foundation raised funds from a skeptical philanthropic community, ran interference with an often resistant bureaucracy, supported residents in strategic planning and projects to clean up the community and get them title to their yards, and oversaw capital projects. Throughout, the project enjoyed the strong and active support of HRH The Prince of Wales.

Our work in Jamaica was galvanized by women. After Michael Black's untimely death, women in the community assumed leadership positions in the Rose Town Benevolent Society, managing strategic planning, organizing workdays, and brokering tensions between Upper Town and Lower Town. Rose Town Foundation director Angela Stultz advocated effectively for the community and focused our attention on the need for social development to come first. She motivated the young people to join our training programs and worked with Jamaican architect Ann Hodges on design and construction issues.

Ann, who was the architect for Island Records president Chris Blackwell both at his family retreat, Strawberry Hill, and at Ian Fleming's former home, Golden Eye, was as facile at preserving the character of vernacular buildings as she was at designing Jamaican resorts, and her contacts across Jamaican society were invaluable. Ambassador Brenda Johnson and Michelle Rollins were essential and indefatigable board members, chivvying reluctant potential donors who didn't believe things could be made better in Kingston, and using their contacts to advocate for the community with the Jamaican government and the international community. Some say that Jamaica is a matriarchal society, and my experience there convinced me that a bit more matriarchy might be very beneficial in the rest of the world.

Perhaps the most profound impact of the effort was the breaking out of peace between Upper and Lower Rose Town. This enabled us to establish building-craft training programs for young men and women from the community, to refurbish a disused chapel as a library and study center for children in the community, and to use the young trainees to rebuild some homes for elderly residents. Community workdays cleared brush and cleaned the infamous trenches, abating the threat of malaria. A timely grant from Britain's Department for International Development enabled seventy-five families to begin obtaining legal title to their properties and revealed that the Jamaican government didn't have processes in place to allow this to happen either quickly or easily.

A grant from the Kuwaiti government funded the installation of a sewer, a water main, and a paved street connecting

Upper and Lower Rose Town for the first time since the center of the community had been bulldozed in the eighties. Local residents were hired on the project, and Prime Minister Portia Simpson Miller attended the opening, prompting some questions about why the Jamaican government had to rely on Kuwait to fund basic infrastructure in inner-city Kingston. Other funding enabled the establishment of carpentry and masonry construction enterprises. A 2014 project funded by Canada enabled a third social initiative, the Rollins Center for Women's Enterprise. The Rollins Center is now housed in a rebuilt building in the Rose Town center. Once a store, it had become the dumping ground for bodies during the wars in the community. After much debate about the building's unhappy

Resident putting the finishing touches on
Rose Town Library, Jamaica. (Credit:
provided by The Prince's Foundation, UK.)

history and the possible presence of "duppies," or ghosts, the Benevolent Society decided that this repurposing would be a positive symbol of rebirth. It hosts not only a women's sewing business but also a market garden.

Housing programs still haven't taken place, but the small interventions have made a difference. Jamaican authorities are now doing a better job of taking responsibility for basic infrastructure, and Jamaican businesspeople now sit on the foundation's board. Taxi drivers will take visitors into the community, and the streets are no longer blockaded to prevent drive-by shootings. Sometimes small matters.

In the end, the lesson I take from Rose Town is not to reject master plans and visions, but to limit their scope. In his influential book *How Buildings Learn: What Happens after They Are Built*, American author Stewart Brand introduced the concept of "pace layering," meaning that different parts of a building—or a city—change at different rates. When applied to civilization, pace layering implies that certain deep structures, like the relationship between a city and nature, or the culture of a city, ought to change slowly, while other activities, like entertainment or retail, shift more quickly and need to be accommodated in a flexible manner within these more permanent layers of the city. We planners should steward nature in the city and sustain culture. At the same time, we ought to absorb and accommodate commerce and fashion, meaning that the city should be robust enough and adaptable enough to embrace short-term shifts in retail or work habits without undertaking structural changes. Infrastructure sets the framework for doing this: whether water, sewer, rail, or road, infrastructure investments shape the city. (See the image of Brand presenting his theory of pace layering in chapter 1.)

Stewart Brand has said, "The fast parts learn, propose, and absorb shocks; the slow parts remember, integrate, and constrain. The fast parts get all the attention. The slow parts have all the power."[2] As planners, we all too often try to get everything right, and we all too often respond to short-term shifts in economic fashion as if they are epochal in nature. City planners have done this in response to retail trends over the last forty years, assembling land and providing roads and subsidies to accommodate a succession of five- to ten-year fashions for selling consumer goods. First came the outdoor shopping mall, then the indoor mall and the festival marketplace. These were succeeded in turn by the big box and out-of-town retail, which are now being supplanted by Amazon and internet shopping, along with a return to neighborhood retail. Each wave has left behind stranded public investment, to the point that a cottage industry has sprung up to redevelop shopping centers that are often less than twenty years old. These so-called grayfields are often abandoned but are well positioned on transportation interchanges and at the center of suburban communities.

There are huge opportunities for enabling small-scale entrepreneurial action not only in the decaying High Streets and abandoned shopping centers but also along highway strips and ribbon developments in established cities and on public lands that were once used for transport or logistics or industry and have now become surplus to requirements. One's first inclination might be to assemble these into big parcels, solicit a master developer, and do a comprehensive plan. However, the experience of my career has led me to believe taking a more incremental approach might be better in the long term, both for the economy and for human happiness.

Chapter 3

Do It Yourself:
An Enduring Idea

D O IT YOURSELF, OR DIY, was a rallying cry for my generation coming up in the seventies. Beginning after the death of the hippie era as a reaction to the commercialization and ponderousness of popular rock music, with its fog machines, stadium shows, and interminable guitar solos, DIY maintained that anyone could start a band, publish a fanzine, or shoot a film.

Frank Gargani's photos in the Los Angeles zine *No Mag* captured the spirit and defiance of the punk and postpunk era, while Nick Modern's *Sluggo* perfectly captured the crazy blend of conspiracy theory, pop culture, and underground music that characterized Austin, Texas, in the days before it became famous as a counterculture capital. My friend Ric Cruz's poster art for upcoming gigs was how people found their way to Austin shows before the rise of alternative weeklies. And a crew of Texas expats founded the *LA Weekly*, where many of the punk scene's habitués, artists, and musicians managed to draw a weekly paycheck. Some went on

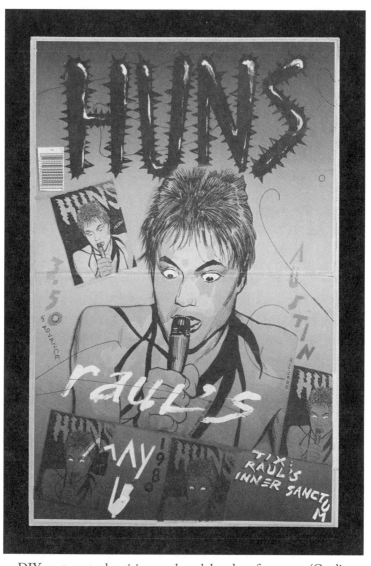

DIY poster art advertising punk rock band performance. (Credit: provided by artist; Ric Cruz; Austin, TX.)

to careers in mainstream journalism, and one even earned a Pulitzer Prize.

Do It Yourself emerged in the latter half of the twentieth century as a reaction to the increasing complexity and specialization of consumer goods—and perhaps to the marginalization of craft in the wake of the Industrial Revolution. DIY looked back to hobbyists and craftspeople for inspiration, drawing from magazines such as *Popular Mechanics* and *Model Railroader* that showed people how to pursue their hobbies and avocations. Launched in 1902 and still going, *Popular Mechanics* may be the granddaddy of this movement. It provides both "how-to" articles on home construction, auto repair, and gadgetry and also reports on invention and technological advancement. Over the years, the how-to industry has focused especially on home improvement, with magazines and television shows promoting everything from carpentry to self-building (as custom building is known in Britain).

In the sixties and early seventies, the countercultural *Whole Earth Catalog* promoted access to tools for the back-to-the-land movement. Founded by Stewart Brand, the *Whole Earth Catalog* aimed to help people create alternative lifestyles and alternative communities, combining ecology, futurism, product reviews, and helpful DIY articles in a large-format paperback book. Produced in Menlo Park in the San Francisco Bay Area, the *Whole Earth Catalog* drew its authors from both the San Francisco and California hippie community and the emergent technology culture of Stanford, Palo Alto, and Menlo Park. As a catalog, it promoted access to tools rather than access to finished products, and this distinction was carefully spelled out from the beginning:

An item is listed in the CATALOG, if it is deemed

1. useful as a tool,
2. relevant to independent education,
3. high-quality or low-cost,
4. not already common knowledge, and
5. easily available by mail.

Stewart Brand and his colleagues saw their audience as being the many communities that were springing up around the United States as hippies sought to try new ways of living. They peddled the catalog through the Whole Earth Truck Store, traveling around to the various communes to both sell the catalog and get ideas for future editions and supplements. The *Whole Earth Catalog* authors distinguished themselves from both the New Left and the New Age. They were interested neither in doctrine nor in mysticism but rather in finding the practical tools needed for mutual self-reliance in systems thinking, shelter and land use, industry and craft, communications, community, nomadism, and learning. As Brand said in a 2017 interview with Chris Anderson of the TED ideas conference, "So the efficient thing to do if you want to make the world better is not try to make people behave differently like the New Left did, but just give them tools that go in the right direction. That was the *Whole Earth Catalog*."

The catalog itself exemplified a DIY aesthetic, as it was produced in-house with the latest technology: Polaroid cameras; IBM Selectric typewriters with different balls for different fonts, obviating the need for typesetters, light tables, and paste-up; and copy machines. Brand and his colleagues were happy to embrace both traditional and vernacular craft and practice, and emergent scientific and technological thinking. Inside the same cover one could find tools for building traditional structures designed by indigenous peoples and instructions for erecting Buckminster Fuller's geodesic domes. Happily pluralist, their criteria were those above all of utility, independence, and quality or cost. This was not too far from the Roman architect Vitruvius's tenets of Commodity, Firmness, and Delight.

Produced under the auspices of the Portola Institute and published by a Berkeley collective called BookPeople, the *Whole Earth Catalog* went through a number of supplements and editions and an interesting cast of contributors including author Ken Kesey, poet and farmer Wendell Berry, and Berry's fellow Kentuckian Gurney Norman. They eventually packed it in with *The Last Whole Earth Catalog*, released in 1974 by mass-market publisher Random House. (Different versions were published sporadically through 1998.)

The *Whole Earth Catalog* had a massive impact on popular culture, especially in California. Its influence was felt in state government during Jerry Brown's first stint as governor in the 1970s, when he appointed *Catalog* contributors such as anthropologist Gregory Bateson, poet Gary Snyder, and architect Sim Van der Ryn to government positions. The *Whole Earth Catalog* was especially influential in its home territory of the South Bay, which was rapidly becoming what we now know as Silicon Valley. All those tinkerers in garages ended up bringing society the personal computer, the internet, and the mobile phone. Apple cofounder Steve Jobs famously commended the *Whole Earth Catalog* in a commencement address at Stanford University this way:

When I was young, there was an amazing publication called the *Whole Earth Catalog*, which was one of the bibles of my generation. It was created by a fellow named Stewart Brand not far from here in Menlo Park, and he brought it to life with his poetic touch. This was in the late 1960s, before personal computers and desktop publishing, so it was all made with typewriters, scissors, and Polaroid cameras. It was sort of like Google in paperback form, thirty-five years before Google came along: it was idealistic, and overflowing with neat tools and great notions. Stewart and his team put out several issues of the *Whole Earth Catalog*, and then when it had run its course, they put out a final issue. It was the mid-1970s, and I was your age. On the back cover of their final issue was a photograph of an early-morning country road, the kind you might find yourself hitchhiking on if you were so adventurous. Beneath it were the words: "Stay Hungry. Stay Foolish." It was their farewell message as they signed off. "Stay Hungry. Stay Foolish." And I have always wished that for myself. And now, as you graduate to begin anew, I wish that for you.[1]

The DIY aesthetic blossomed again in the mid-1970s with the punk era, as musicians and artists reacted to the growing commercialization of both music and art by forming bands and record companies and coming together to open studios, galleries, and clubs. Unlike the DIY of the *Whole Earth Catalog*, punk DIY was a radical simplification of what was seen as the bloated excesses of popular music and art, perhaps exemplified best by progressive rock and stadium rock, promoted by big record companies in huge concert venues and overplayed on the radio.

In contrast, punk DIY was fast, loud, and simple. Learning two or three chords was enough to start a band, and—borrowing from Burroughs and Gysin—a pair of scissors, a stack of magazines, and a pot of glue was enough to make the gig poster.

Cult band the Minutemen sang, "We were fucking corn dogs" who "drove up from Pedro." The title of that song, "Our Band

Could Be Your Life," inspired a book that collected the stories of indie bands in the eighties and early nineties, as the DIY punk aesthetic gave way to Indie. Indie was a credo for record labels and bands that existed apart from the corporations that dominated the music business in those last days of music as a physical product.

Recent years have seen similar interest in DIY homebuilding and development, from the popular tiny-house movement in the United States to self-building in the United Kingdom. Increasingly, neighborhoods and community groups are planning their own futures through groups like Better Block and tools like Tactical and Lean Urbanism in the United States and neighborhood planning in the United Kingdom, where over 2,000 neighborhoods and parishes have organized to develop their own plans. And perhaps the most compelling evidence of DIY is in the informal settlements that characterize urbanization in the Global South.

This active effort on both sides of the Atlantic to encourage ordinary people to become small-scale builders and developers has been encouraging. Once again, this reflects the history of city building. While Chicago's great lakefront parks and City Beautiful plans get lots of attention, for example, much of Chicago was built out by recent immigrants in the form of two- and three-flat buildings, where the builder/owner lived in one unit and rented out the others.

DIY has always been something of an oppositional movement, and indeed, recent years have seen a marked decline in small enterprise and small-scale development in both the United Kingdom and the United States. This shift appears to be driven by market consolidation, by the disproportionate burden of regulation on small-scale businesses, and by the tendency of government economic development professionals to seek to attract large employers or to enter into development agreements with large developers for large parcels. All of these combine such that the big get bigger and the small fade away.

The scale of the problem can be easily seen in both the United States and in Europe. According to the Kauffman Foundation, which tracks trends in entrepreneurship in the United States, the business start-up rate today is half what it was in the 1980s, declining from 165 start-ups per 1,000 firms in 1977 to 85 per 1,000 firms in 2016.

The number of small builders in the United Kingdom has declined dramatically as publicly traded homebuilders have consolidated and government programs after the recession have helped the larger companies more than the smaller ones. Smaller builders also experienced a credit squeeze in the wake of the 2008 recession, as, unlike the five largest homebuilding companies, they were not considered too big to fail. In 2017, the House Builders Federation of Great Britain reported, "There has been a long-term decline in the amount of SME house-builders, falling 80 percent over the past 25 years.... During the financial crisis there was a very steep decline with one-third of them folding between 2007 and 2009."[2] Denial of credit, inability to access land, and challenges for small players in the planning process were cited as continuing problems in a recent study by the Institute for Public Policy Research, which described the three problems as one interrelated "toxic triangle."[3]

The United States has seen a similar collapse of small building and retail, with the Institute for Local Self-Reliance finding that the number of small construction firms declined by 12,000 from 1997 and 2012, while the number of local retailers dropped by 40 percent in the same period.

A similar trend has been seen in community banking, which historically has been the lender that has financed Main Street businesses and property development in the United States. Community banks are often called "relationship banks," as their smaller scale and higher capitalization allows them to focus on customer relationships and to lend capital based on intimate knowledge of both their customers and the local business climate. Historically, they have provided over half of small business loans and a large share of lending for local property development in the United States, particularly for housing. And the evidence is that their better local knowledge has resulted in lower default rates than real estate lending by the bigger institutions—a 3.47 percent default rate for community banks versus over 10 percent for large banks. Despite the advantages, however, recent years have seen a decline in community banking and a consequent decline in lending for small business and small development. This decline has been driven by a number of factors, including bank consolidation and mergers, and, ironically, the requirements of the Dodd-Frank bank legislation, enacted after the Great Recession ostensibly to deal with large bank conglomerates.

A 2015 study by the Harvard Kennedy School found that "community banks' share of US banking assets and lending markets has fallen from over 40 percent in 1994 to around 20 percent today. Particularly troubling is community banks' declining market share in several key lending markets, their decline in small-business lending volume, and the disproportionate losses being realized particularly by small community banks." The Harvard study found that "larger banks are better suited to handle heightened regulatory burdens than are smaller banks, causing the average costs of community banks to be higher. . . .

Policymakers should also examine simpler capital rules and various rule exemptions for community banks."[4]

There may be a huge latent demand for small building, especially in existing cities where the market has improved and vacant properties and vacant lots abound. Developers Jim Kuman and John Anderson have been the Johnny Apple-seeds of the movement to recruit small-scale developers in the United States, crisscrossing the country and putting on boot camps to teach the rudiments of undertaking a development project. Their Incremental Development Alliance is encouraging architects and planners and others that development is not an arcane art and that there are pathways to building smaller projects that are open to all. These include the use of conventional home mortgages to finance a fourplex, so long as the owner lives in one unit and rents out the rest.

In Britain, architect and developer Roger Zogolovitch urges everyone to become a developer in an engaging little book entitled *Shouldn't We All Be Developers? The Case for the Independent Developer*. Meanwhile, urbanist Kelvin Campbell and his son Andrew, with the help of Rob Cowan, have been chronicling small-scale action through their Massive Small Collective. This web- and print-based project aims to "mobilise people's latent creativity, harnessing the collective power of many small ideas and actions to make a big difference." The Massive Small Collective argues for delegating decisions to the lowest competent level: "In the public sphere, responsibility and accountability must be devolved to the lowest levels—fundamentally changing the scope and purpose of practice from being reactive controllers to becoming co-creative enablers."[5]

At the same time, there has been a big push in England to empower local communities as expressed in the Localism Act, which empowers neighborhoods to organize themselves and develop neighborhood plans. These plans can be adopted by referendum after a lengthy process and a government inspection, and then they must be incorporated into local plans by the borough or local authority. Over 2,000 such processes are underway in England, both in rural and small-city parishes and also in big cities, and many of them are doing a careful job of identifying small-scale sites.

There is a separate but related movement for self-building, also called custom building, and government has been taking steps to make it easier. The rate of self-building in Great Britain is far below that in Europe, and the reasons have much to do with the dominant role of bigger builders in finding, optioning, and taking land through the planning process. This has meant that there is little land available for self-builders, alongside the challenge of dealing with a planning process geared for big sites and experienced builders, and a finance system that doesn't anticipate individuals or small collectives engaging in construction.

Government is tackling these challenges in different ways: requiring local authorities to maintain a register of people interested in self-building as well as a register of available sites, amending planning rules to make it easier for self-builders and small builders to get permission, and allocating portions of government property for small builders. The expertise gap remains to be tackled, however.

A few inspiring DIY projects have begun to emerge. In the suburban London borough of Barnet, the Older Women's Co-Housing Group (OWCH) came together to design and build twenty-five self-contained flats with a shared communal kitchen, dining area, meeting room, and gardens, of which seventeen flats are owned by their occupants and eight are for social renters. Their story is one of incredible perseverance, as the group first began meeting in 1998, with construction finally completed in 2016. The group met and organized for several years before Hanover housing took an interest and helped to find a site. Planning permission took eighteen months and was finally granted in 2013. The group worked closely with the architects at Pollard Thomas Edwards through a collaborative design process. The resulting scheme is delightful, and the members have undertaken to harvest lessons learned and document them online and in a short film, hoping to make the DIY process easier the next time.

The social enterprise developer Igloo has promoted self-building on a site called Heartlands in Cornwall. Here the emphasis is on making it easy for people to build a house. Rather than designing it themselves, Igloo allows purchasers of a plot (for which they have provided services and infrastructure)

OWCH cooperative home. (Credit: courtesy of OWCH;
Barnet/London, UK.)

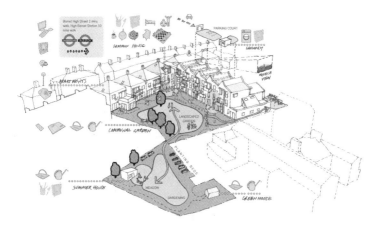

Architect's sketch captures OWCH spirit. (Credit: courtesy of Pollard Thomas Edwards LLP; London, UK.)

to choose from designs by six different architects. These range from homes by established kit manufacturers to a seriously funky straw-bale house, all of which can receive customized details, fittings, and decoration.

So far the number of such schemes has been modest, but the policy changes are still bedding in. Interestingly, there seems to be heightened interest in self-build in the Southwest of England, where the *Telegraph* reported in March 2018 that 7.9 percent of homebuyers were purchasing buildable plots rather than completed homes.

Of course, self-building a new house is only one form of DIY, and there is evidence that more Britons are interested in starting their own small business, remaking their home, or adding additional units on their land than has been the case for many years. Some credit the millennial generation for the explosion of start-ups, and certainly the dearth of permanent employment has led both Generation X and the millennials to make their own gigs. The profusion of food trucks and food carts, pop-up shops, and traders selling artisanal goods and foodstuffs at markets is an indication of the demand for DIY. And so, I might add, is the prevalence of white vans and skips, which in the United States would be called dumpsters, on my modest terraced street in North London, signifying the prevalence of DIY movers and renovators!

An American study recently estimated that in 2017, food trucks had become an industry with US$2.7 billion in annual revenue, but it warned that the costs of regulation were inhibiting further growth. The report *Food Truck Nation*, by the US Chamber of Commerce Foundation, found that food truck operators face an average cost of regulation of US$28,000 and that the average food truck operator has to deal with forty-five different government requirements, over more than thirty-seven business days, to get a permit. One operator in Austin told researchers that it shouldn't be harder to get a food truck permit than to open a brick-and-mortar restaurant.[6]

Making the transition from pop-up to established retail gets even more difficult, however, and the complexity of processes geared for and partly designed by corporations and businesses with multiple outlets and a central staff infrastructure is a problem, and one that we will deal with in detail.

There is a sort of conundrum in applying the idea of DIY to cities, for cities are inherently places where people come together to do things: to trade, to exchange goods and ideas, to meet and mate, and to form communities. But the enduring appeal of DIY is surely not the solitary pursuit of a loner existence but the coming together with neighbors, colleagues, or friends on a new business, a new building, or a new service, in contrast to the increasing consolidation and market concentration that characterizes the global economy.

Do It Yourself might better be called Do it Yourselves, as Stewart Brand observed in one of the *Whole Earth Catalog* updates, in 1979:

> For example, is it preferable to be dependent on institutions we don't know, and which don't know us, or on people, other organisms, and natural forces that we do know? . . . I'm betting that abandonment of illusions of self-sufficiency will free us to accept and enjoy local dependency, by preference. And since our world is increasingly cultural, and proportionally ever less physical, the meaning of "local" is not geographic, at least not only.

For me, Do It Yourself never meant do it alone, whether it was starting a food cooperative in my early twenties, a performance series in my thirties, or a new nonprofit in my forties. Rather, DIY always meant finding some like-minded colleagues and having a go. Over time, that seems to have gotten progressively harder, even as the demand and opportunity for Do It Yourselves has grown and grown.

Chapter 4

Doubling Up:
Lessons for Cities from
Life during Wartime

with Scott Bernstein

C ITIES AT WAR CAN BE DESTROYED, as were Beirut, Aleppo, and Dresden, or partially destroyed, as were London, Berlin, Baghdad, and Kabul. After the war these cities have to rebuild, and how they do so has been the subject of much study and debate.

Cities also have to change to meet the demands of wartime, by preparing for attack and by accommodating rapid influxes of workers into urban areas or, on the other hand, evacuating civilians to the countryside. How cities have adapted to the dramatic crises resulting from conflict can help us think about dealing with current challenges such as addressing housing shortages, accommodating refugees, combatting flooding and other natural disasters, and adapting to climate change.

I became interested in this issue when I began to think about the affordability crisis in London and many other successful cities in the developed world. Experts estimate that London is only building about half of the 50,000 new homes it needs each year. The average price of a London home in the fall of 2019 was £472,000 (approximately US$608,000),[1] which compares unfavorably to an average salary of £52,000 (approximately US$67,000) for an Inner London resident.[2] When this is coupled with a predicted growth in population to 10 million by 2030, one realizes that a lot of people are coming to a London without a lot of new housing. Where do they live? Lots of ink has been spilled to tell the stories of people stacked in sheds and garages and of awful landlords, but hard numbers about overcrowding and predatory landlords are hard to find.

Anecdotally, though, one hears of four millennials sharing a one-bedroom flat. Where are they going, and what can we do about the fact that the market is underdelivering housing and delivering luxury investment flats that don't correlate to the need on the ground? By some estimates, 30 percent of new Inner London housing is bought by offshore investors and remains unoccupied. According to the latest US Census, 60 percent of residences in a fourteen-block area of midtown Manhattan were "seasonally vacant" between 2013 and 2017. Other US cities also have high rates of absentee or investor ownership: approximately 40 percent of homes in Phoenix and Las Vegas and only 30 percent of homes in Miami are owner-occupied.

Successful cities in stable economies are being hit with the triple problems of unaffordable housing, undersupply of new homes, and new homes being bought for investment, driving up prices and further tightening supply all over the world. This crisis is manifest in New York, San Francisco, and Portland, Oregon, in the United States; Toronto and Vancouver in Canada; and Sydney and Melbourne in Australia.

I decided to look at some historical precedents in order to think about how cities can deal with rapid population growth in times when housing supply is constrained. I remembered an exhibit years ago at the National Building Museum in Washington, DC—an interesting museum in an amazing Victorian edifice that once housed the US Patent Office. The show was mostly about the transformation of the US economy and the American way of life after World War II, but it also showed how the seeds of that transformation were sown during the war. Washington, like many other cities, became a center of the war effort during World War II, and people moved there from all over the country. Many of the migrants were civilian workers, and the capital region doubled in population during the war era.

This happened at a time when materials and workers were needed for the war effort to build ships, tanks, trucks, and airplanes, so prewar housing programs were canceled or severely curtailed. How did the city cope? I discussed this problem with the most indefatigable researcher I know, longtime colleague Scott Bernstein, cofounder of Chicago's Center for Neighborhood Technology. We have been collaborators since the early nineties, and I knew this question would stimulate Scott's curiosity.

Over the course of the next several months, Scott trawled through records in university and government libraries and kept coming across the phrase "doubling up," referring to the accommodation of new arrivals within existing housing stock.

And in fact, it appears that this is exactly what happened. Single-family homes took in a lodger, big homes became boarding houses, and people shared flats and hotel rooms. Alleys were developed with alley flats, the precursor of today's buzz trend, the "accessory dwelling unit" or "mother-in-law or granny flat." The government facilitated all this by eliminating or reducing planning and building regulations that had been put in place to prevent just such an outcome in single-family neighborhoods.

During the Second World War, Washington, DC, grew from a population of 663,000 in 1940 to 881,000 in 1945, with a net in-migration of 49,000. The greater Washington region grew as well, doubling in population. At the same time, in order to dedicate resources to the war effort, the government had imposed restrictions on new housing construction. According to *Fortune* magazine, "The War Production Board . . . follows the theory that each pound of nails used for housing is wasted."[3]

Beginning in 1940, government and industry commissions began to look into the problem of a housing shortage. In February 1941, the *Washington Post* reported on a Works Progress Administration survey that found fewer than 2 percent vacancies in Washington, DC, along with especially high rents. The survey found that the vacancy rate had dropped from 5.4 percent to less than 2 percent in a matter of months.[4]

Some housing was built—barracks for soldiers, and multi-family housing in suburban Alexandria—but it fell far short of meeting the demand. Holly Chamberlain observed in "Permanence in a Time of War: Three Defense Homes Corporation Projects (DHC) in the Washington DC Metropolitan Area" that perhaps the effect was greatest in the Washington area, where the lack of sufficient housing was severe. Over 7,500 units—more than half of the almost 11,000 units the DHC built as garden apartments, single-family dwellings, and dormitories in thirteen states and the District of Columbia—were in the Washington area. Chamberlain goes on to describe a dormitory with 6,160 rooms for both civilian and military government "girls" at Arlington Farms, Virginia; ten low-rise buildings of 610 units each near Arlington National Cemetery with canteens; two privately built apartment-house developments providing more than 8,500 homes, and within DC itself, a privately constructed 250-room hotel with shuffleboard, wienie roasts, movies, dances every Friday night, and a dating bureau; and the Meridian Hill Apartments, government-financed but privately built with 634 rooms for 725 girls.[5]

Most of the new construction was outside of Washington, and overwhelmingly the population increase within the District was handled by doubling up; the balance was from expedited development and from redefining the goal of "public housing" to "war worker housing." The federal government made a deliberate effort to help the local Washington, DC, government lower barriers to doubling up. In practice this meant two things: loosening regulations that had been put into place to restrict rooming houses and boarding houses, and encouraging householders to take in workers by renting spare rooms, converting porches to rooms, and building what are now called accessory units. Federal policy in this regard was explicit: the National Housing Agency (NHA) explained that it would obtain wherever possible the use for housing accommodations of the maximum number of rooms and family accommodations in existing structures, convert existing spaces to make apartments and rooms available for housing accommodations, and disapprove new war housing construction in any locality except to the extent that the housing needs of the locality could not be met by these measures.[6]

The effort to encourage converting larger buildings to boarding or rooming houses reversed a trend that had discouraged this type of housing, popular in the 1800s and early 1900s but later stigmatized. Zoning had been used to prohibit rooming houses in residential neighborhoods as a result of campaigns to stamp out overcrowding and what was called the "lodger evil." Lodgers were characterized as a threat to family peace and morality. The antilodger campaign succeeded, with the proportion of homes with lodgers in larger cities dropping from 20.6 percent in 1910 to 8.5 percent in 1940.[7]

Government had to work to reverse this discrimination against multiple occupation, both by loosening rules and by removing the stigma with public relations. It became a patriotic duty to house war workers, and contemporary newspaper and magazine articles promoted the idea, portraying both war workers and their accommodation with families and in boarding houses sympathetically.[8] Even the *Washington Post*'s society pages got into the act: a 1943 article featured a Mrs. Eldridge Jordan, who had opened her home to friends to help ease the shortage. Her boarders included Mrs. Henry L. Roosevelt, widow of the secretary of the navy, who had decided to lease out her own Washington, DC, home for the duration so that it could accommodate more people. Another guest was a woman working at the British Purchasing Commission who happened to be the daughter of a prominent admiral. The message was that if society women were taking in lodgers, then it was fine for middle-class homeowners to do the same.

Another *Post* article featured eight British Navy Wrens who decided to double up by living together, family-style, in a five-bedroom brick house. Sadly, the girls lost their first maid, who thought the house was haunted, but a replacement named Geneva turned out to be an excellent cook.

Not only was there a concerted effort to make sharing and boarding socially acceptable; there appear to have been multiple campaigns to induce homeowners to modify their buildings to accommodate more people. One such campaign focused on the conversion of porches to bedrooms, with multiple wartime newspaper stories making the point that this was an easy way to help the war effort and make a few dollars at the same time. "Where housing accommodations are inadequate to meet the needs of industrial workers, many old-fashioned but spacious porches could be enclosed to make additional rooms. In most cases such change would not only bring in regular rentals but improve the appearance of the property." The helpful article goes on to note, "Work of this kind may be financed [through] the FHA's [Federal Housing Administration's] Repair for Defense program."

Hollywood got into the act as well, as part of the film industry's propaganda effort in support of the war. The 1943 Columbia Pictures comedy *The More the Merrier* focused on the Washington, DC, housing shortage, and the misadventures of a woman (Jean Arthur) and two men (Charles Coburn and Joel McCrea) forced to share a small apartment. Of course, the film ends happily with the army sergeant getting the girl. Other titles in this genre included *Government Girl*, *The Doughgirls*, and *Johnny Doesn't Live Here Anymore*. Documentary shorts also chronicled the issue, often featuring the lives of young women working in the war effort.[9] All these productions served to normalize sharing and doubling up, and to make running and living in shared accommodation seem a patriotic part of the war effort.

Federal policy also focused on the conversion of existing homes to accommodate additional residents by adding units with new construction, subdividing existing dwellings, and adding rooms and bathrooms for lodgers. Multiple federal programs facilitated such expansions. For example, in most cases, conventional lending periods were not long enough to allow the costs of such conversions to be amortized. In response, the FHA extended the amortization period for loans it insured under its title 1, easing the credit problem. In addition, government architects were made available at no cost through the Federal Home Loan Board to help property owners draw up conversion plans.

Local barriers to home sharing and taking in lodgers were addressed as well. Over the previous half century, local policies had discouraged lodgers and boarding houses by zoning many city neighborhoods for single-family occupancy. Planners realized that this inhibited converting large homes for multiple occupants during wartime, so there was an effort to encourage local government to loosen these rules. The federal Homes Utilization Program was established to encourage conversion, and one of the issues it addressed was loosening zoning restrictions for the duration of the war. In 1942, the National Housing Agency issued extensive guidance in this regard, targeting single workers, couples, and families with particular recommendations that would support doubling up.[10]

For Washington, DC, which as a federal district was governed by a committee of the Congress, a 1942 bill permitted boarding houses in previously restricted residential areas for the duration of the war, subject to obtaining a certificate and meeting fire safety regulations. The bill passed within months, with a proviso that such boarding homes should not be permitted if they were likely to cause blight.[11]

The plight of single women coming to Washington as war workers received special attention, and plans were made to build dormitories for them. A *New York Times* article noted

Greeting the new boarding house roommate, 1943. (Credit: Library
of Congress, Prints & Photographs Division, FSA/OWI Collection,
LC-DIG-fsa-8d25536.)

that women workers didn't want to live in faraway suburbs, as
they wished to be in the District itself, "where the action is."
Official estimates in 1942 proposed that of the 20,000 new
female workers, 3,000 could be accommodated in boarding
houses, 900 in two now single-room-occupancy hotels in
Washington, and the balance in "blueprints . . . recently authorized by Congress." Wartime DC was said to have over 10,000
lodging houses.

Underpinning the concerted efforts to promote doubling up, provide finance for conversion, and remove barriers by loosening regulations, there was the constant threat that the government could act under war powers to billet war workers in private homes. In a remarkable, somewhat tongue-in-cheek speech in 1942, President Franklin Roosevelt reminded the public that he had this power and suggested that "parasites" with no real role in the war effort should move out of Washington for the duration. He made a point of referring to his friends who had "twenty-room mansions on Massachusetts Avenue."

Federal authorities were also keeping an eye on close ally Great Britain, where wartime housing needs were being met by extensive requisitioning of private homes and billeting of war workers. As a contemporary account of the British approach by the Federal Home Loan Board found, "By far the largest number of war workers and others have been accommodated by billeting either on a voluntary or compulsory basis," noting the wide powers given to the government to commandeer homes and place people in private residences. These powers were used both to manage the evacuation of women and children from cities during the Blitz and to station war workers near industrial areas. The Federal Home Loan Board reports contained such statements as "Building new homes will not be enough."[12]

One Works Progress Administration memo estimating the extent of the doubling-up phenomenon was based on a survey of civilians who moved to Washington, DC, after October 1, 1940, and who were still living there in November 1941. There were 36,300 "families" (households) living in DC who met the dates and residence criteria, containing 36,800 workers (basically one worker per household) and a total of 51,700 persons. Of these households, 78 percent were composed of one person,

DC Population
1936-1950

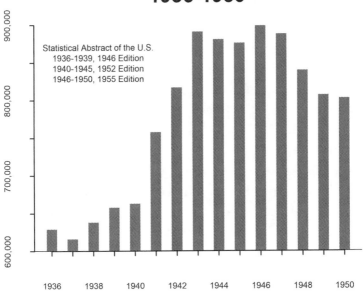

Population growth and decline in Washington, DC, in the World War II era. (Credit: created by Peter Haas and Scott Bernstein, Center for Neighborhood Technology.)

were composed of two, 10 percent had three or four, and 2 percent had five persons or more.[13]

The memo found that only 15 percent of the 36,300 households occupied their own dwelling; 85 percent were "sharing a dwelling with others," and 3 percent were living in hotels. Of one-person households, 94 percent were sharing a dwelling with others, while only 39 percent of multiperson households were sharing.

Thus, the growing number of people coming to DC to help with the war effort was largely accommodated within the existing housing stock by repurposing public housing as wartime housing and by doubling up, with existing households being converted to flats and families taking in lodgers. It is likely that much of the population growth was housed in informal lodging, and the strategies identified—targeted use of housing finance innovations, support for streamlining of local regulations, and simply looking the other way—were the lean way to get there quickly enough to matter.

Washington, DC, in World War II offers a landmark case of urban resilience. There were three main techniques for accomplishing this objective: loosening local regulations that prohibited lodging houses and multiple occupancy, providing financial and technical assistance to property owners wishing to convert their buildings in order to accommodate war workers, and public relations efforts to erase the stigma around boarding houses and convince the public that doubling up was patriotic.

The federal government in its own indirect way aided and abetted this by coming up with flexible financing terms, paying for housing centers to match willing property owners with job- and home-seekers, and publishing official guidance on ways to modify existing local rules. Architects were made available to advise on converting buildings in compliance with fire and safety regulations.

Local governments all over the country relaxed zoning prohibitions on multifamily dwellings and enabled property owners to register new boarding houses, usually for the duration of the war effort. Washington, DC, enacted its version in 1942.[14]

Moving the idea of the lodging house from a reformer's "evil" to a necessary asset was a signal accomplishment. News articles, society page features, newsreels, feature films, and even presidential speeches were employed to convince the public that doubling up was not only moral but patriotic, and practical advice, moral suasion, and humor were all used.

In the end, the effort worked.

The end of the war resulted in a decanting of the wartime population, an immediate urban renewal push (aided by Cold War politics when the Soviets released a picture of DC slum alley housing, prompting congressional hearings),[15] wholesale slum clearance in the District, and rapid growth in the suburbs. Beginning in 1956, the interstate highway program provided quick access to the new suburbs, and the Veterans Administration loan program and depictions of the joys of suburbia in film and the emerging medium of television together created a suburban explosion that boosted the US economy and decimated its urban areas. In many ways, it was a good thing that the Washington, DC, region met its wartime requirements by recycling and repurposing its existing housing stock, for after the war ended, DC's population quickly dropped by almost 200,000.

The experience of Washington, DC, during the Second World War certainly demonstrates that cities and their people can adapt to crisis and that there is inbuilt resilience, or slack, in existing cities. In normal times there is little incentive to deploy that extra capacity, as taking in lodgers may be both inconvenient and financially unnecessary. Exigencies can bring this capacity into play, and a combination of bottom-up individual action (DIY), government facilitation, and PR can work wonders.

Regulations are often designed to fix a place in time—for instance, as a middle-class single-family-home neighborhood—and protect a perceived quality of life or limit diversity in ways demanded by residents. In times of stress, these rules are a barrier to responding in a way that meets the crisis, whether it is wartime housing or neighborhood decline or a shortage of affordable housing.

Are there lessons from the wartime experience that can be applied today to cities facing problems of housing supply or affordability? London provides a timely case.

Almost everybody agrees that London faces both a housing supply problem and an affordability crisis. The supply problem is demonstrated by comparing housing construction at its peak with the numbers generated today. In the fall of 2019, new housing starts were down more than a third from a year previous, and half the all-time high in 1972, with starts of multifamily housing down 30 percent.[16] And most observers seem to agree that supply shortages drive prices up, causing the affordability crisis.

But what if London had only an affordability crisis, and the supply numbers were an artifact of lobbying by homebuilders to ease planning restrictions on new housing projects and for government to stimulate demand through various incentive programs? After years of demand stimulation and planning reform, the number of permitted developments is actually up, but the number of housing starts is much lower. By and large, in London the new starts are being sold into the investment market.

So supply increases but slowly as London's population continues to grow. Where are all the people going? We hear stories of garages and sheds crammed full of Eastern Europeans, of millennials sharing flats, and of young people remaining at home with their parents longer and often returning. In a compelling feature for the *Guardian* in May 2017, Anna Minton found that "Ealing may have as many as 60,000 occupants in illegal structures, and Slough borough council, which deployed planes equipped with thermal imaging equipment in an effort to spot them, may have as many as 6,000 beds in sheds."[17]

According to a 2014 survey by the Office for National Statistics, "In London more than 1 in 10 households (11.3 percent) were overcrowded, and about 4 in 10 households (39.3 percent) had the recommended number of bedrooms (zero-occupancy rating)."[18] All this data is used to demonstrate the need for more homes, but there is little correlation between the needs of this population and the units that homebuilders are producing. Part of the answer to this unmet need must be to get local authorities building housing again, but another part of the story has to do with what I would call urban recycling.

There is evidence that housing demand is being met in London through the same doubling up that occurred in Washington, DC, during World War II. According to Max Hutchison at sparerooms.co.uk, there are 19 million empty bedrooms in owner-occupied property in the UK, and 2016 saw a quarter of a million people advertising rooms for rent.[19] London has the highest proportion of homes with six or more occupants and saw the largest proportional increase between 2001 and 2011 at almost 50 percent, according to the Office for National Statistics.[20] At the same time, just under half (49.4 percent) of London households had spare bedrooms in 2014, demonstrating lots of additional housing capacity.

Allowing conversions of owner-occupied homes to accommodate lodgers or create an additional flat as permitted development would be a further incentive to put these empty bedrooms to use, generating needed revenue for many people with substantial equity in their homes but limited income. Homeowners who rent a room in their home are given a powerful incentive under British tax law, as they can earn up to £7,500 per year renting out furnished rooms in their principal residence free of tax. This benefit could be better publicized, in the way that the US government promoted sharing during World War II.

It is well documented that more and more families are living as intergenerational households, with adult children remaining in the family home for much longer. The notion of allowing conversion of owner-occupied homes to accommodate a parent or a child as permitted development is a way to encourage urban recycling without allowing slumlords to develop substandard accommodations.

England has a regulatory subsystem for registering what are called houses in multiple occupation (HMOs), restricting their number and ensuring they meet health and safety standards. The vast majority of the overcrowded "beds in sheds" exist in the gray economy, outside of these regulatory schemes. A house in multiple occupation has at least three tenants not of the same household who share a kitchen, toilets, or bathrooms. The more regulated category of large HMOs must be at least three stories high, with at least five tenants sharing facilities. The regulations require gas safety inspections annually, fire safety measures, ample cooking and bathroom facilities and rubbish bins, and adequate common and individual space.

The standards seem sensible, so the problem with overcrowded beds in sheds is one of enforcement and assisting homeowners to come into compliance. If policy were to encourage people taking in lodgers, sharing households, and running HMOs, such assistance would be a big part of the process. While it might be costly, it is less costly than building new affordable housing, for this kind of shared lodging was once the mainstay of housing affordability.

Sharing may be more attractive than it once was, owing to postrecession housing costs and possibly also to the more urban lifestyles of the millennial generation. The opening of a number of catered shared buildings for millennial workers, replete with game rooms, cafés, and activity directors, harks back to some of the big Second World War complexes in Washington. These "co-living" developments are cheaper than having one's own flat but more private than sharing an apartment, offering extensive communal facilities to make up for the small individual spaces. The co-living developer Collective and the venerable housing charity Peabody are both renting such living accommodations to young Londoners. The developer Pocket is building one-bedroom apartments for "London's city makers. They are compact, and priced at least 20 percent lower than the open market for . . . the city makers who contribute so much economically, socially, and culturally to our city, yet are unable to buy their first home."[21] Similar companies have emerged in the United States, among them the co-living operators Common and Pure House.

Much attention has been paid to the supposed problem of under-occupation by aging baby boomers in London, with proposals to encourage them to sell their homes to people starting families and move to serviced apartment buildings in city-center locations. Evidence shows that most don't want to leave their neighborhoods, and so a report by former London mayor Boris Johnson's urban design advisors recommended that converting one's home to accommodate lodgers, build an accessory unit, or house a caregiver be considered permitted development not requiring planning permission.

This trend toward doubling up appears to be prevalent in the United States as well, driven less by a shortage of housing and more by the economic instability experienced by many young people. America is long on built space, except in the very hottest housing markets such as San Francisco, Seattle, and New York

City. Vacancies are high not only in residential but in commercial spaces; the annual change in households is very small, on the order of 1–2 percent over a very long period of time.

Here's Zillow's definition of a doubled-up household:

> We define a doubled-up household as one in which at least two working-age, unmarried or un-partnered adults live together. Under this definition, a 25-year-old son living with his middle-aged parents is a doubled-up household, as is a pair of unmarried 23-year-old roommates. This definition captures the households that under different circumstances contain adults who could or would choose to live apart. Some individuals do choose to live with others for companionship and camaraderie. But the relatively lower individual incomes of employed adults living in doubled-up households and the strong relationship between rental affordability and the share of adults in doubled-up households over time and across metro areas suggests that sharing living expenses is more than a matter of taste.[22]

The Zillow researchers estimate that in 2014, 32 percent of all adults (age twenty-five and over) in the United States lived in doubled-up households by their definition; the numbers were higher in "hot market" areas and in ports of entry, consistent both with affordability explanations and with observations that the majority of immigrants live in such places: "Large metro areas with the highest share of adults living with roommates include Los Angeles (47.9 percent), Miami (44.5 percent), New York (42.5 percent) and San Diego (39.7 percent)."[23]

None of this necessarily favors smaller towns or larger cities. With more transparency and awareness that doubling up is happening, smart places will be the ones that lower the barriers. A few years ago, the *New York Times* carried a story about a

Ramshackle Rose Town house being restored. (Credit: provided by The Prince's Foundation, UK.)

Rose Town house given new life. (Credit: provided by The Prince's Foundation, UK.)

Incredible Edible Todmorden mural with admirers. (Credit: courtesy of Incredible Edible Todmorden Community Benefit Society; Todmorden, UK.)

The author and Prince Charles considering a plan with graduate fellows, 2010. (Credit: provided by The Prince's Foundation, UK.)

Trinity Buoy Wharf before renovation. (Credit: courtesy of Eric Reynolds; Urban Space Management; London, UK.)

Aerial view of Trinity Buoy Wharf in 2019 with its many uses. (Credit: courtesy of Eric Reynolds; Urban Space Management; London, UK.)

DIY straw-bale house in Central Texas. (Credit: courtesy of
Annie Borden; Dripping Springs, Texas.)

homeowner in Queens who converted his basement, illegally, into a decent apartment for under $10,000; not only was he fined, but the city made him tear the unit out.[24]

Cities faced with a variety of challenges could benefit from policies and programs that favor doubling up. Poverty, costly housing, pressures from migration, and the need to accommodate people during war or after natural disaster are all situations in which a safe and organized program to promote shared accommodation makes sense.

Such a policy might include eliminating zoning and planning barriers to people living together, assisting homeowners with converting their residence to take in lodgers in a way that meets building regulations, providing financial assistance through mortgages, and forming nonprofit housing agencies that own and operate boarding houses and single-room-occupancy hotels. Because of the stigma created around these useful forms of housing by well-meaning reformers in the last century, these programs need to be accompanied by marketing and PR efforts targeting not just busy millennial web workers but also single adults, recent immigrants, and older homeowners, outlining the financial and social benefits of doubling up, just as Hollywood did for the government girls in the Second World War.

This effort would have a number of benefits, extending far beyond making homes more affordable for many. Doubling up exploits the built-in slack, or resilience, in cities, saving both financial capital and resources. *Dilbert* cartoonist Scott Adams said it well, though with tongue planted in cheek, after trying to build an eco home: "The greenest home is the one you don't build. If you really want to save the Earth, move in with another family and share a house that's already built."[25]

Chapter 5

Slack Is a Good Thing

I N THE URBAN CONTEXT, Doing It Yourself exploits
an important characteristic of evolving cities and culture, and
that is the reservoir of *slack*—an indication of resilience—in
both human and physical capital.

One of the most influential independent films of the last
half century was called *Slacker* (1991). The first film of the
independent director Richard Linklater, it depicted a group of
friends and acquaintances of the director in late-eighties Austin, Texas. Perched midway between university and responsible
adulthood, Linklater's protagonists were making art, spinning
wild conspiracy theories, and subsisting without a lot of money
in a series of warehouses, ticky-tacky apartment buildings, dive
bars, and streets and porches. (Full disclosure: Linklater and
many of his cast were close friends of my wife's, and we became
friends as I came to know them over twenty-five years.) Shot
on a shoestring, the film moved from one character to another,
depicting a postpunk scene full of people—slackers—who did
a lot of talking, a lot of hanging out, and a good bit of art.

Through *Time* cover stories, in-depth *New York Times* articles, and follow-on films like *Clerks* and *Reality Bites*, the media

Local actors in memorable scene from the movie *Slacker*. (Credit: courtesy of Detour Inc.)

used *Slacker* to define a generation. To me, it also defined a quality of the cities where I grew up in the period between the urban dystopia romanticized in the Kurt Russell vehicle *Escape from New York* (a stereotype seemingly still prevalent in the minds of Donald Trump and his former attorney general Jeff Sessions) and the glitz of today's second Gilded Age.

Before TV shows like *Seinfeld* and *Friends* made cities trendy for young professionals, declining city neighborhoods were cheap places for artists and bohemians—what we now call "creatives." It was said that these young people delayed growing up in order to experiment with starting a band, writing a film, opening a restaurant, or launching a computer company.

And that's what *slack* is all about—the space to experiment, the room to grow, and the ability to do so without a venture capital angel, a deal with a media company, or a trust fund.

Notably, there are two parts to slack: affordable places and human capital. In this case, affordability is the chance for someone to exist in a milieu with others like them, where rents aren't too high, cultural experiences can be had, and there are gathering places that allow people to connect.

The second part of slack is the chance for people to take time off before getting on with a career or starting a family, in order to try something different. In the past, there were always artists or bohemians—whether children of privilege or of the middle class—who filled this niche. These are the people who made up the Lost Generation of Americans in Paris after the First World War and the Bloomsbury set in England. It wasn't until the period after the Second World War that the idea of a youth culture came into being, as well as the notion that the young might reject the paths of conformity laid out for them by society. In the sixties this was tied to revolutions, civil rights, antiwar and environmental activism, psychedelics, and the back-to-the-land movement. In the late seventies, this rejection became broader with the punk movement.

"The point of [the film] *Slacker* is that these people *aren't* slackers," Austin journalist Louis Black says. Longtime editor of the alternative weekly *Austin Chronicle* and cofounder of Austin's famed South by Southwest Music Festival (known as SXSW), Black is a champion of the hardworking creative community that inspired Linklater's film. "People make films, have blogs, are in bands," Black says. "They're slackers because they don't have jobs."[1]

I asked Richard Linklater whether slacking is an essential component of becoming a creative person or artist. He was unequivocal that it is, and that slackers earn their position by personal sacrifice and attracting disapproval from society. He responded,

> To have any chance of finding your voice in this world and defining your true passion, I think it's absolutely necessary to spend some significant time unattached to any market forces. Being divorced from the workforce and the official society can help you see things clearly. Of course, no one's going to offer you these conditions willingly. Opting out is a process of earning it by saving and buying and sacrificing your way out and then having the strength to put up with whatever negative judgment that goes with it.[2]

Linklater worked on oil rigs in between periods of working on his first film, and he famously financed it with credit card debt.

Ivan Stang (born Douglass St. Clair Smith), whose humor project the Church of the SubGenius came out of Texas in the eighties and has gotten a new life online in recent years, made slack the center of his satirical religion. But there was an underlying current of serious intent behind the absurdity: "For some of us," he explains, "slack is not actually sitting around watching TV with a beer in hand. For some of us, slack is doing the work, but the work we wanted to do. I basically am now doing what I'd be doing anyway, so I feel real good about my situation."[3]

Downtown Manhattan musician Marc Ribot argues that the late twentieth century was the first period when working-class young people had the chance to participate in this kind of creative scene. In an interview with the online magazine *Guernica*, Ribot, who earned his chops playing with Tom Waits, John

Lurie, Allen Toussaint, and Elvis Costello alongside his own work in avant-garde jazz and Cuban music, said that New York in the eighties allowed working artists to survive. "In the eighties, when you didn't need a ridiculous amount of money to get an apartment in New York, you had working-class people who could participate in the music scene. Venues paid. CBGB paid, at least in the beginning, and working-class musicians—even those with drug habits—managed to find work."[4]

So in this sense, slack is two things: underutilized or vacant space, cheap to rent, in which to both live and work, and also untapped human or social capital. The happy combination of the two may be what makes for a "scene"—or, in the language of people like urban theorist Richard Florida, "creative capital." One had only to look at Manhattan and London and Los Angeles in the late seventies and eighties to see this happening in Tribeca and the East Village, in Shoreditch, Spitalfields, and Brick Lane, and in downtown LA, Echo Park, and East Hollywood.

This idea of slack has a footing in both popular culture and management economics. In the context of a business enterprise, organizational slack is the difference between total resources and those payments or costs required for the conduct of the firm's business. The concept of organizational slack was first outlined by Richard Cyert and James March in their 1963 book *A Behavioral Theory of the Firm*. They theorized that, in a firm, "slack operates to stabilize the system in two ways: 1) by absorbing excess resources, it retards upward adjustment of aspirations during relatively good times; 2) by providing a pool of emergency resources, it permits aspirations to be maintained (and achieved) during relatively bad times."[5]

According to Cyert and March, "to keep the various groups in the organization, payments had to be in excess of what was required for the efficient working of the firm. The difference between the total resources and the necessary payments is called the organizational slack. In conventional economic theory, organizational slack is zero, at least at equilibrium." Cyert and March posit that organizational slack plays a stabilizing and adaptive role.

Literature on slack argues that there is a conflict within firms between global pressure for productivity and efficiency and the need to preserve some slack, as slack is positively correlated with innovation. Too much slack, and the firm is neither innovative nor efficient. Too little slack, and there are no resources available for improvement and innovation.

Slack is akin to the principle of redundancy in systems theory. Like slack, redundancy turns out to be a good thing, though it is popularly believed to be a synonym for waste. Redundant systems have multiple pathways, reducing the possibility of bottlenecks and the impact of failures in one part of the system. Redundant systems, such as the internet, can adapt and learn. This may also be the function of slack in society.

Applying this to the city, slack exists in many postindustrial cities in the form of former factories and goods yards, warehouses, disused storefronts, former railway lands, and so on. All of them are ripe for repurposing. When cities were not a target of global capital for investment, those lands—which planners call "brownfields" to distinguish them from undeveloped "greenfields"—were the places that attracted people on the margins, like artists, immigrants, and gays. They could live and work in warehouses and lofts, abandoned buildings and repurposed shipping containers. They still live in those areas in growing cities in the Global South.

Planning scholars including Timothy Pattison and Phillip Clay have identified a four-step process of regeneration: at first,

Artist spaces in Container City at Trinity Buoy Wharf, London, UK.
(Credit: courtesy of Eric Reynolds; Urban Space Management;
London, UK.)

disinvested neighborhoods are occupied by those oblivious to
risk—artists, musicians, and slackers; then these neighborhoods
become the target of what are called risk-aware settlers—often
gays or people buying their first home. Those newcomers in turn
make those neighborhoods attractive to what planner Andrés
Duany calls "the dentist from New Jersey"—risk-averse investors capitalizing on the property value created by the so-called
pioneers. And finally come government and institutional investors, creating a sort of climax state of urbanism, with luxury flats,
chain retail, or Class A office space. At each stage, land values
in such neighborhoods increase, and those dwelling there stand
to either cash out by selling or be forced out by the rising tide,
depending upon the security of their tenure.

In recent years in cities that attract global investment, like
London, New York, San Francisco, Toronto, and Vancouver,

that four-step process has been replaced by a two-step or even one-step process. Close-in neighborhoods go directly from being occupied by the poor alongside artists to becoming targets for public-private partnerships to develop the area. The land is often assembled into large parcels and sold for development through a bidding process, attracting large-scale investors or public-private partnerships. A development plan is prepared, and so-called meanwhile or temporary uses are "curated" to get people used to coming to the area.

Filmmaker Linklater, who has seen the population of his home base of Austin, Texas, more than double since 1990, notes the impact that this accelerated investment has had on Austin's artistic scene: "I think economics are unfortunately deeply intertwined with any art scene—as in, if no one can afford the rent, the scene disperses. Community is important, and it's up to the artists to make it happen and find a place for themselves somehow, somewhere. It's never easy and has only gotten harder in the rapidly growing cities like Austin."[6]

Austin built its reputation as a creative city, with the SXSW music, film, and now interactive festivals and a legendary hospitality toward live music and musicians. Linklater himself, along with director Richard Rodriguez, did a lot to promote independent filmmaking in the area. Michael Dell's decision to base his computer company in the metropolitan area helped cement its reputation as a tech hub. And rising housing costs and congestion in California stimulated a migration to the city that for a time called itself "the Third Coast."

This four-step process of gentrification ends with city districts becoming targets for luxury housing and investment buildings that can be promoted to offshore investors. This in turn drives up land values and prices as landowners speculate that they can convert their property in this way. The flow of investment capital into cities, whether from publicly traded homebuilders, private investors' banking vehicles in Guernsey or Barbados or Cyprus, or sovereign wealth funds, has driven a motivation to eliminate slack, driving land prices up beyond the feasible.

In terms of urban real estate, slack is replaced with property as a holding container for capital and excess wealth. The consequence is unequal development, as well as a lack of capacity to adapt to changing economic circumstances. This has an effect on human capital, as the space for experimentation is denied to working-class and even middle-class people, as it is simply unaffordable to remain in the city without a full-time job or without subsidy.

Slack for creativity, entertainment, and the arts also exists in cities as temporal slack, or what has been called the twenty-four-hour city. A growing number of cities are recognizing that a significant amount of economic activity occurs from 6:00 p.m. to 6:00 a.m. and that the people participating in it are often the young, educated, creative, and entrepreneurial—the kind of people you want in your city. From Vancouver to New York to Tokyo, municipal governments are exploring how to nurture the nighttime economy that can be the new competitive edge for global cities. Amsterdam was the first to select a "nighttime mayor" whose job is to support the nighttime economy and enable it to coexist with the other half by managing rowdiness and maintaining public safety, with improved lighting and expanded transportation, planned events and festivals in public spaces, extended hours for licensed facilities, and a crew of trained but friendly "hosts" to keep the streets calm at night. In London, where 1.6 million people usually work weekends and nights, a "Night Czar" appointed by the mayor and a Night Time Commission are working to identify the policies needed to support the "sustainable development of London at night." That includes encouraging DIY music venues to replace the pubs and clubs that have closed in recent years because of skyrocketing rents.

Slack can also be found in smaller cities and towns, often with cheap housing, abandoned or declining commercial and industrial areas, and reasonable access to a big city with an arts tradition being squeezed by the influx of global capital. But few of these cities as yet have the agglomeration of young people that makes a scene, and efforts to establish a market town as the next Shoreditch or the next Brooklyn have seldom been successful.

Slack also exists in the still significant parcels of public land in many cities formerly used by railroads, freight yards, or government facilities. If public policy supported keeping such property in the public domain and making it available for small-scale enterprise on a long-term lease, there could be a base for small business and start-ups even in the most go-go city economy. Unfortunately, there is a fervor for disposing of this kind of property as soon as possible, as expensively as possible, and in as few transactions as possible, generally to the largest company interested.

In London, for example, a 2017 opinion piece in the *Guardian* described the national government "selling off public land at an unprecedented rate" to plug budget holes, while also claiming that the "disposal of public land to the private sector" would increase the stock of housing. However, only one in five new homes to be built was classified as "affordable," and many of these proposed developments would be luxury housing only. In Washington, DC, a twenty-four-acre parcel along the Potomac River was sold by the city to a private developer for "an array of high-end hotels, entertainment venues, shops, restaurants, and apartments," some selling for almost US\$3 million, according to the *New York Times*. (In this case, as part of the sale, the developer agreed that one-fourth of the housing units will be listed as affordable.)

All this is happening at a time when the changing nature of work may create a huge surplus of human capital. Much has been made recently of the plight of the white working class in formerly industrial and mining communities, as well as the tie between their joblessness and lack of prospects and the politics of resentment and scapegoating practiced by the US president Donald Trump and the UK's Nigel Farage. J. D. Vance's memoir *Hillbilly Elegy* is but the first of a number of popular efforts to explore the decline in prospects for the rural white working class, and to define it as a phenomenon in and of itself. Vance's book was followed by scads of earnest reportage in the hinterland.

Of course, this more-recent media discovery of rural poverty is overlaid on persistent structural unemployment in communities of color, stemming from both racial policies and the decline in manufacturing jobs and union protections. While white resentment may be its own thing, the structural economic condition is crosscutting and profound, and the politics of stoking resentment toward communities of color and immigrants is an American political tradition dating back to the founding of the republic.

An even more profound shift in the nature of work has been taking place over the past decade. Dubbed the "gig economy" by some, it represents two significant trends in the nature of work and in the scale and capacity of technology.

First, an increasing share of work is "nonstandard" (NSW), meaning that it is not full-time permanent employment. According to the Organisation for Economic Cooperation and Development (OECD), nonstandard work is a significant and growing share of all employment in the developed economies of the OECD:

> The share of NSW in many OECD countries' workforce is significant and growing. Across [twenty-nine] OECD countries the average of the NSW share in total employment is 33 percent and contains almost equal portions of temporary jobs, part-time work, and self-employment. Without counting permanent part-time work, the category that seems least likely to occur as PW [Permanent Work], the average share of NSW is 22 percent in these countries.[7]

The second trend is growth in freelance employment, as companies increasingly shift to hiring contractors rather than employees and people have to work on multiple short-term projects to earn a living. Estimates of the scale of freelance employment vary widely, due to differing definitions by government statistical agencies. One of the most credible estimates has come from a partnership of the Freelancers Union and the company Upwork, who together have done surveys of the scope and extent of freelancing in the United States. Their 2016 survey of 6,000 Americans found that 55 million people, about 35 percent of the workforce, were freelancing: "Almost half of working Millennials (47 percent) freelance, more than any other generation."[8] As of 2018, according to the OECD, 15 percent of people in the United Kingdom were self-employed.[9]

Not only are the conditions of employment changing, but the nature of work is changing, too. Many believe that we are entering a period of the greatest change in work since the Industrial Revolution moved the working population from the farm to the factory. Automation and robotics in both manufacturing and service industries are increasing and projected to pick up pace in coming decades, restructuring or eliminating many types of jobs. In 2016, the OECD found that across OECD countries, 14 percent of jobs are at high risk of being automated, while another 32 percent of jobs will change significantly because of automation. This is a conservative estimate.

For generations entering the workforce now or in the near future, the outlook is indeed murky. No longer are high school or university graduates likely to get a job with an employer and stick with that job for years, earning benefits and a company-provided pension. That scenario, except in some government employment, began to erode in the eighties and has continued to do so.

The US Bureau of Labor Statistics estimates that anywhere from 3.5 percent to 15 percent of those working less than thirty-five hours per week would work full time if they could.[10] (The variance depends on the reason for working part time; for example, if a parent works part time because quality childcare is not readily available, that does not mean that full-time work has not been offered but it can mean that with a better set of childcare options the parent would choose full participation in the workforce.)

Many millennials view automation as inevitable, with a Deloitte survey finding that "40 percent see automation posing a threat to their jobs; 44 percent believe there will be less demand for their skills; a majority believe they will have to retrain (51 percent)."[11]

Younger workers have responded to this change with realistic shifts in strategy and expectation by building a portfolio of part-time jobs, by initiating and completing projects such as pop-up shops or catering gigs, and by learning to value happiness over security. They also seek flexibility within full-time work in order to pursue larger goals, to find space for volunteering, and to work from home or work nonstandard hours.

This attitude frustrates many of my baby boomer friends, who look at this generation and see people who don't have commitment or staying power. But that may get the wrong end of the stick, as young workers are making the best of a work world that is radically different from that faced by people who entered the workforce in the seventies, eighties, or nineties.

My millennial friend and colleague Charlotte Castle is a case in point. Charlotte is the daughter of a close friend from university days. Like many of her generation, Charlotte has pursued a career defined more by her values than by job security. Now working for the City of Philadelphia organizing its pedestrian priority and safety program Vision Zero and its annual Philly Free Streets event, Charlotte says the theme of her career has been a focus on social equity, first as a student visiting Malawi, then as an AmeriCorps worker with the homeless, and later with the West Philly Tool Library, a unique organization helping people get the resources they need to repair their homes.

Charlotte has responded positively to the gig economy: "On paper, I am a City official, but I also am an artist, a barista, an urban farmer, an educator, a volunteer coordinator, a homeless services supporter, a student, a mentor, and much, much more. I believe that the gig economy inspires me and my peers to take risks—and that these risks will continue to fuel more and more diverse and dynamic perspectives throughout the workforce."[12]

If we roll the tape forward a decade or two, we will be looking at developed-world economies where there simply is not enough paid employment to go around, and where there are also likely to be huge gaps between the skills needed and the skills available in the workforce. In other words, a lot more people will be working part time, and not by choice, and others will be imagining new ways to make ends meet.

Many argue that the answer to this challenge is twofold: better and more targeted job training in the jobs that may emerge as automation increases, and the provision of a guaranteed basic income, replacing the dole with a stipend for everyone.

When I was in high school, futurists were confidently predicting the advent of the four-day and even the three-day workweek as automation and the Green Revolution in agriculture ushered in an era of plenty where the drudge work was done by machines. Of course, that hasn't happened. People who have full-time jobs work harder and longer than ever, and people who don't have permanent employment are often eking out very marginal livings. The great wealth that has been created has not been broadly shared, going most of all to those in the financial sector.

But in another way, those predictions of a future without so much labor are coming true, albeit without the safety net or the "rising tide" envisioned by most back then. I had a look at some of these near futures to see if there were any lessons or ideas we might apply today.

The great New Wave science fiction writer Samuel R. Delany posited a useful idea in his 1984 book *Stars in My Pocket like Grains of Sand*. Set in a distant future where gender is fluid and humanity inhabits thousands of worlds, the book's protagonist is one Marq Dyeth. Marq has two vocations: Job 1 is as an industrial diplomat where he is called on to transfer technologies between worlds on an occasional basis; Job 2 is as a teacher in a school within his intentional community. Delany thus expresses the idea that one might have a vocation and also a commitment that extends beyond volunteering to being an integral part of community-building. As Dyeth says, "I like my work2 a lot, as well as my work1. And I like my work1 a lot."[13]

This change is happening, and it behooves mayors and local officials to accommodate it by identifying ways to make or preserve physical slack in their cities, either to attract or to retain young people and people starting up enterprises.

They also need strategies and policies to grow the collaborative sector—charities, co-ops, co-working spaces, studios, and workshops—that creates the spaces that enable these young creatives to flourish.

And the need for slack in urban property is profound, for changes in the nature of work have been profound and have created an even greater reservoir of human and community capital without much opportunity to engage itself.

If we are looking for a future with lots of slack in people's lives, we need to find spaces for them to live and work, and also places to create a scene or platform. Back in the day in Manhattan, it was CBGB's, the bar that birthed the punk music scene, or Max's Kansas City. In LA, it was the Masque, Al's Bar, and the American Hotel. In Austin during Richard Linklater's era, it was the Austin Film Society and clubs like Raul's and the Beach. Each of these cities also had cheap living spaces, coffee shops and bars that let people linger, and usually a university or cultural institutions that created a draw for the young.

Scenes are platforms for trying out new ideas, for being both spectator and performer, inventor and investor, lender and borrower. People often observe that, since the invention of the internet and the instant availability of all information, there is no longer an underground. Richard Linklater doesn't agree: "The underground is the incubator for the new. And it's just fun to be a part of—extending that middle finger to the status quo mainstream. And a scene can pop up anywhere there's a group of passionate folks that care enough about their community and want to make it happen. It's important to be questing for the world you live in to correspond with your desires and passions."[14]

The ongoing restructuring of the economy is opening up the capacity for people to pursue projects of their own, to start short- or long-term enterprises, to volunteer, or to make art or music or films. The kinds of projects that emerge from this kind of slack can be diverse and inspiring.

Charlotte Castle introduced me to one such project with which she became involved in a diverse Philadelphia neighborhood. Established to enable people to improve their homes themselves, the West Philly Tool Library lends tools to homeowners and renters seeking to decorate, rehab, or expand their residences. Not only is this a responsible use of resources, as an individual often needs certain tools only once, but it is also an empowering one, enabling men and women alike to improve their own living situations.

I visited another unique project in Lancashire, England, a few years ago in my capacity as head of Prince Charles's architectural foundation. The prince has long been a supporter of both community revival and healthy food and gardening, and he visited the town of Todmorten on the royal train to showcase the Incredible Edible Todmorten project. Plagued with persistent underemployment, Todmorten could have been like many towns in the north of England that are dependent on the dole and characterized by multiple generations out of work, with poor diets and rising obesity and morbidity. A group of residents resolved to do something different, conceiving of the entire town as an edible garden and planting fruit and nut trees and vegetables on disused land and street sides across the city. In this way "slack" land became productive land, city dwellers became gardeners and collaborators, and healthy eating became a trendy thing.

Granville Island, technically a peninsula in Vancouver, was a scene. Originally conceived as an industrial redevelopment project, it became an arts and creativity hub, with an art school, an outdoor market, street and arts fairs, chefs, and live music. But since Granville Island itself is crown land (that is, owned by the Canadian federal government), it was never going to be controlled long-term by the committee of artists who ran it for decades. In 2017, the Crown Mortgage and Housing Corporation, which manages the island on behalf of the government of Canada, announced a 2040 plan, the results of a public engagement process that had input from 10,000 stakeholders and members of the public. The island will be overseen by a council of CMHC and local representatives and has added a water park, an elevator to the mainland, and other attractions. Though the council will support the arts with below-market rents for artist spaces and short-term rentals to let potential tenants test the waters, my friend Anthony Perl reflects that it has become too bureaucratic to allow the "freewheeling creativity" that true scenes and incubation spaces require. But its brief flowering as a space for the arts to experiment and interact with one another and the public presents a visible ideal that other such places can strive for.

Chapter 6

When Meanwhile Becomes Permanent: Eric Reynolds and London's Revival

I
N 1970, NO ONE COULD HAVE FORESEEN that the former railway yards and warehouses at Camden Market would become one of London's most visited destinations, or that Spitalfields, a market in the East End of London, would host lunchtime crowds of City bankers and shoppers at trendy boutiques.

The discovery and reuse of vacant buildings and incremental revitalization of urban neighborhoods makes cities more adaptable and resilient. Large building projects, whether master-planned urban districts or high-rise residential towers, can't change their use in the same way. So, as with the mantra "reduce, reuse, recycle," urban revitalization is tapping into the inherent resilience of cities. Doing it in an incremental, organic way builds a stronger urban ecosystem.

Everywhere in the world's cities, small, funky workspaces are fully occupied, yet cities are not making more of them. Except for individual and exceptional entrepreneurs, the usual approach to an underutilized asset has been to put a new iconic building beside it or to retain the facade and build something inside to attract retail chains, instead of figuring out how to clean it up, provide some social and business infrastructure, and get occupants into it.

Trinity Buoy Wharf and the Tea Building in London, Birmingham's Custard Factory and Jewellery Quarter, and Bristol's Tobacco Factory are all good examples of the organic approach. The English coastal town of Folkestone got it right by putting an iconic arts building in last, after attracting an artistic community with low-cost space in older buildings. In each case, the revival was spearheaded by an entrepreneur with drive, patience, some undervalued space, and the will to pursue the projects incrementally. All of these projects create jobs, and all are founded on a yeasty mix of small and medium enterprise and creative and cultural assets. There is a lot to learn from them, and a lot to learn from community entrepreneurs.

The Custard Factory in Birmingham is a former manufacturing quarter, overseen for many years by urban entrepreneur Bennie Gray and his son Lucan. Too often, historic rehabilitation projects begin with a complete—and costly—building makeover and then seek to attract tenants to a space now embedded with cost. Gray began by making only the improvements needed to make the space suitable for tenants and then sought to attract them by providing an atmosphere that encouraged them to congregate there. As the leasable space became fully occupied, Gray expanded to other buildings and then sought grants to ensure that the heritage value of the buildings was not lost.

Architect and developer George Ferguson has done this kind of urban homesteading in Bristol in the West of England with the Tobacco Factory, and he extended his ideas about lively, arts-based regeneration as Bristol's first elected mayor. In the United States, people can point to Dallas's Deep Ellum, Manhattan's SoHo and TriBeca, and Chicago's Wicker Park as examples of districts that have gone through this cycle of urban renewal, beginning with festivals, entertainment, and the arts. But many of these have lacked the long-term management strategy found in the British projects cited above.

In contrast to this incremental approach, most local government growth planning seems to focus on attracting big sheds on big sites, building business or industrial parks, and thinking in a zoned way rather than seeing jobs as part of the mixed urban ecosystem. Small-business space is seldom retrofitted or built, as that must be done speculatively and, while it can more than pay for itself, does not produce large profit margins. Some of this is the consequence of planning and building regulations, but mostly it is due to a preoccupation with large business, chain retail, and a sort of big bang theory of economic development. This thinking ignores the fact that most job growth occurs in small businesses.

Arts-and-crafts-based revitalization and urban markets are often seen as a stage in the gentrification process, and developers and local governments often refer to the occupation of unused commercial space by artists and creatives and the programming of events and markets to activate an area as "meanwhile" uses, until something better or something that attracts higher rents comes along. However, such uses are essential to the creative, knowledge-based city, providing a launchpad for innovation, an attraction for the young, and a characterful reuse of the existing and valuable historic urban fabric. The approach to retaining this character and this activity is different from the usual development model; it is more akin to gardening or forestry than to industrial agriculture, as revealed by a closer look at one project in East London.

I first heard of Eric Reynolds's project at Trinity Buoy Wharf in the early 2000s, though I didn't visit until much later. The old wharf-and-warehouse complex was directly across the River Thames from the absurd and emblematic Millennium Dome, one of New Labour's flagship big projects. (Before-and-after photos of Trinity Buoy Wharf can be found in the centerfold.) The wharf's historic lighthouse hosted a smaller and more particular millennium project, Brian Eno's Long Player, a piece of music composed with a computer program and some Apple iMacs that was designed to play for 1,000 years. The Long Player prefigured Eno's, inventor Danny Hillis's, and Stewart Brand's Long Now Project to build a 10,000-year clock and was a similar attempt to adjust the horizons of our thought beyond the short term.[1]

Trinity Buoy Wharf was the wharf and workshop for the Corporation of Trinity House, chartered by Henry VIII to maintain beacons and lighthouses on the Thames. It was also the place where a lot of invention in navigation and hazard warning took place, and its buildings were as much inventor workshops as factories. A number of Victorian buildings still survive, including the lighthouse. In the late nineties and early 2000s, it was directly in the path of New Labour's regeneration of East London with the full panoply of demolition, glass towers, and so-called iconic development projects.

I knew little about Trinity Buoy Wharf when I was invited to accompany Prince Charles and The Prince's Trust CEO Martina Milburn for a visit hosted by Eric Reynolds, who had masterminded the development of the site as a home for the arts

Trinity Buoy Wharf lighthouse, site of the Long Player. (Credit: courtesy of Eric Reynolds; Urban Space Management; London, UK.)

and education. The visit was prompted by Reynolds's decision to bequeath his interest in the project's leasehold to The Prince's Trust, Prince Charles' charity dedicated to helping young people.

I had seen Eric Reynolds at conferences and seminars, and I knew of him as the developer of the markets and stalls at both Camden Lock and Spitalfields Market as lively mixed-use trading centers, attracting Londoners and tourists alike with their diversity, funkiness, and historic settings. In 2010, Reynolds characterized his approach as distinct from that of the usual property developer, noting "the difference between property development in a structured way, as opposed to property development as husbandry—more akin to market gardening than bricks and mortar."[2]

At Camden Lock Market, Reynolds and partners Peter Wheeler and Bill Fulford took up a lease of disused railroad property just next to the canal in Camden Town in 1973. Beginning with a Sunday market—a day when most of London was closed—they gradually built up both an ecosystem of traders and a market of shoppers who came for the locally handcrafted goods, the food, and the music. Camden Market has become known worldwide and is a stop for most young visitors to London, but when Reynolds began building out the market, it was an altogether more interconnected affair. "There was a golden period," Reynolds remembered when I met him one rainy late-summer day at Trinity Buoy Wharf, "when every trader either made their wares themselves or bought them from the person who made them."³

Reynolds, whose then wife, the British Olympian June Paul, handled the food vendors, took an improvisational approach to managing the market. He built racing yachts during the week

Camden Lock before revitalization, circa 1973, London, UK. (Credit: courtesy of Eric Reynolds; Urban Space Management; London, UK.)

and hauled them up to the roof on weekends when the market took place. They needed people walking along the canal towpath to come into the market when they heard the live music, so they made a gap in the wall—with proper technique but without asking. When the need emerged for a proper music venue in the area, Reynolds and his architect set out the levels for the new Dingwall's building on the site and took their design inspiration from nearby buildings. This began Camden's trajectory as the home of Britpop. For the Camden Lock team, heritage was part of the appeal, but these were rough industrial buildings, meant to be used and adapted. It is doubtful that the project would have been viable if today's more precious grant-driven and procedural approach to heritage had been followed.

Eric Reynolds surveying activity after early stages of renovation of Camden Lock. (Credit: courtesy of Eric Reynolds; Urban Space Management; London, UK.)

Spitalfields before repurposing. (Credit: courtesy of Eric Reynolds; Urban Space Management; London, UK.)

In addition to Camden, Reynolds's company took on a lease for Spitalfields Market. Unlike Camden, which had been railroad and shipping lands, Spitalfields had been a market for hundreds of years. With the departure of its traders to a new location in the sixties, the Corporation for London began to think about long-term reuse of the site. They retained Reynolds to manage it as a different kind of market in the interim.

Reynolds took a short-term lease and set about activating the site, with a goal of appealing to and attracting both customers and businesses from within a two-mile radius of the East London market. The local blog *Spitalfields Life* described the result this way:

> Eric sees 1994 as the apogee of this period of the market, when the place flourished with an authentic vigorous life that

had a momentum all of its own. And many have affectionate memories of this time in Spitalfields, when community events coexisted alongside sporting contests and concerts, when the place was full of artists' studios, when a model train ran round the perimeter, when hot food of all kinds could be bought from scruffy wooden huts and [the kinetic sculptor] Rowland Emett's glorious fountain was the centre of this crowded hub-bub, which became a meeting place where everyone enjoyed an equal sense of ownership.[4]

After Reynolds's leasehold of the Spitalfields Market was terminated, the Borough undertook to develop the site further. It raised the rent on many long-term tenants in 2005–6, attracting restaurant chains and fashion brands such as Burberry and AllSaints and building a shiny new retail area next to the old buildings. The market area was reduced in size and

Street scene at Spitalfields Market. (Credit: courtesy of Eric Reynolds; Urban Space Management; London, UK.)

diversity, and the traders became less unique. Vintage clothing traders, for example, couldn't compete on price with the volume pricing of the fast-fashion brands. Camden was undergoing a similar redevelopment, with a multimillion-pound restaurant/nightclub called Gilgamesh and physical improvements, but it proved more resistant to the clean-up efforts.

In both cases, something was lost. The capital value that Reynolds had created with his husbandry led the site owner to seek to maximize income by raising rents and building new structures that could attract standard retail and food tenants, as opposed to the smaller businesses that had fit happily into smaller spaces with perhaps less-than-ideal tenant improvements. It always seemed to me that something essential was lost in the transition and that this was a result of a failure to understand the essential qualities of the place and of applying a standard development model to a nonstandard place. If small works, it must be temporary, so the thinking goes, and big would be better. Along with saving the buildings, heritage-led regeneration has to be about saving the life in the buildings, and often that must mean keeping the place in a state that doesn't fit the standard model that the occupier and the valuer are looking for.

Knowing this history, I was intensely curious to see what Mr. Reynolds was up to at Trinity Buoy Wharf. It turned out that Reynolds had also reset his deal structure after the great successes at Spitalfields and Camden had been deemed to be temporary or "meanwhile" uses, good enough to attract activity but to be succeeded by "higher-value," more-mainstream uses. But that was only revealed as I directed questions to Reynolds and his colleague John Burton from his firm Urban Space Management in the margins of the visit with HRH The Prince of Wales.

The usual entourage accompanied Prince Charles: a private secretary from Clarence House, the Royal Protection officers, and the representatives of his charities, in this case Martina Milburn, of The Prince's Trust, and myself, representing his urbanism and architecture charity The Prince's Foundation for Building Community.

Trinity Buoy Wharf is downriver from both Westminster and the City, and our short voyage from Embankment Pier exposed both the beauty of historic and some contemporary development along the riverbank and some egregious examples of new builds from the eighties through the present day. After the quiet trip downstream, we were met at the wharf by a noisy claque of the royal press corps and their photographers, along with a receiving line of the key people on Eric's team. The first stop was Brian Eno's Long Player in the Victorian lighthouse, still chugging away with now-vintage Apple computers. It set the tone for what we were to see, the reuse of historic buildings for contemporary use, mixed with lower-capital-cost new buildings aimed at small businesses, craft workers, and artists.

We visited tenants, including the scenery workshop for the English National Opera, a primary school, a diner, and artists and craftspeople. Since 2000, the artists' workspaces were accommodated in Container City, a series of modified shipping containers stacked a few stories high and arranged around an elevator core.

Unlike the short-term arrangements at prior projects, Reynolds and his company, Urban Space Management, had secured a long-term (125-year) leasehold interest in the property from the London Borough of Tower Hamlets, saving it from the threat of what in the United Kingdom is called "regeneration," which often involves wholesale or partial demolition. This long tenure ensured that the uses could be sustained over time and that artists, craftspeople, and educators could afford to remain. The leasehold interest is assigned to the Trinity Buoy Wharf Trust, which in turn dedicates 25 percent of its income to subsidizing and promoting arts activities on site. Reynolds's company, Urban Space Management, manages the estate and handles leasing.

Trinity Buoy Wharf is a great combination of heritage, funkiness, and smart strategy, and by all accounts it is a great place to study or to work. Soon after our visit, the University of the Arts, a behemoth arts school that has gobbled up most of the smaller arts institutions in London and is now housed in a bland white whale of a modern building at King's Cross, announced the "rationalization of its educational offering." This meant that, having ingested a number of excellent independent arts colleges, it now planned to eliminate many of their programs, which it viewed as duplicative or niche. One of these was the Art Foundation course at the Byam Shaw School of Art, one of the last introductory courses that took seriously the mission to provide young artists with a solid foundation in artistic skills and disciplines prior to their specializing at university.

The tutors from the course appealed for help to Prince Charles and Director Catherine Goodman of the Royal Drawing School, one of The Prince's Charities, and they in turn appealed to Eric Reynolds to help find a home for the course at Trinity Buoy Wharf. Trinity Buoy Wharf was able to accommodate the course with favorable terms, and so we made a second visit to the project with Prince Charles, Catherine Goodman, and some philanthropists.

By all accounts it has been a successful partnership. Students and tutors alike enjoy the atmosphere and appreciate being cheek by jowl with more-established artists. The infusion of young artists gives the wharf a solid anchor tenant and is a source of vitality in the day-to-day life of the place.

In addition to the Royal Drawing School and the English National Opera, tenants now include the Faraday School, the Thames Clippers (a river bus service), the University of East London, the Big Draw (a national charity dedicated to promoting drawing), and Long Player, along with a diner and many artists and craftspeople in the shipping containers. Recent additions to the building stock have included Clipper House, a building recycled from the Broadcasting Studios at the 2012 London Olympics. Trinity Buoy Wharf has also become popular for events, including weddings, and regularly plays host to art installations.

Trinity Buoy Wharf is a special place, filled with life and organized so that it can endure—unlike so many revitalization projects that are homogenized by later investment and "upgrading." By making only the improvements needed as they are needed for immediate occupation and use, and by avoiding outside capital that brings with it pressure to be paid back in a relatively short period of time, the developer has been able to take the long view. And by securing what amounts to permanent land tenure, he's been able to sequence his use of the space and support creative and meanwhile uses on an ongoing basis, maintaining an income stream that supports the whole. While Eric Reynolds and his company Urban Space Management are singular, and perhaps even heroic, the experience at the wharf need not be unique. It's not unlike what Judi Barker did with her tenants at the Barker Hangar. There are some important lessons that can be drawn from the project and applied elsewhere.

For example, it is instructive that all of the projects I've described, from Camden to Spitalfields to Trinity Buoy Wharf, took place in underused historic districts, either markets or workplace/warehouse buildings. The approach employed by Reynolds and his colleagues was not the usual one of developing a careful conservation plan that looks to meet the highest standards of heritage practice and then applies for grants or tax credits to meet the gap between the income from the intended use and the cost of the conservation work. Instead, these projects did the upgrades needed to accommodate artistic, creative, or communal retail uses, making the most of the historic character of the buildings but bringing them back into productive and income-generating use as quickly as possible. These were not, for the most part, buildings of special architectural merit, and hence the typical approach of combining high design and high conservation was not employed. The same strategy was employed at the Santa Monica airport and, on a much smaller scale, in Rose Town.

This method of simple adaptive reuse as quickly as possible could be employed a lot more frequently if conservation officers and planners understood that this was a more feasible way to reuse many older structures without triggering a massive change in the built environment.

"Meanwhile uses" need not be only temporary. They can form a vital part of the city, playing host to start-up businesses, to creative industries, and to educational institutions. They can exploit the underlying resilience of the city by reusing its adaptable historic fabric, by tapping into the creativity of craftspeople, artistic institutions, and small business, and by integrating lower-cost new builds alongside reused historic structures in a sensitive way.

All of this can happen if one takes the approach, suggested by Eric Reynolds, of urban husbandry, caring for the asset and the users of the asset, rather than the contemporary economic development model of highest use equaling best use. Reynolds characterizes his approach in this way: "*Meanwhile* is developer-speak for short-term income or marketing and brand building. If the right sort of owner is in the equation, 'meanwhile' can and should be an evolutionary process making possible an early start to make use of the space." He notes that landowners should be more willing to engage in these sorts of ventures, as the underlying land value is not at risk in any way.

A funky mix forms the ground floor of the creative economy and is often poorly understood by economic development professionals, who have approached areas like London's Shoreditch / Tech City with plans to attract big tech companies and build large buildings. This ignores the fact that the success of the area has been due to its lively mix of work and live-work spaces alongside pubs and coffeehouses, the tight urban grain of the streets that promotes exchange, and the small, affordable buildings, which are not large enough for retail chains.

But the successful revitalization of older neighborhoods or sites will increase the value of the underlying land, and this will stimulate landowners to seek higher rents or capital gains through comprehensive redevelopment. When they do so, they are often driven by the standard model and by their consultants toward attracting mainstream tenants, meaning chains/ multiples, and these will require substantial capital investment in glass, steel, and amenities, along with much larger floor plates.

Trinity Buoy Wharf offers one way out of this problem. By obtaining a long-term leasehold interest and investing that interest in a trust with charitable aims, Reynolds is able to ensure the longevity of the land uses on the site. And by deeding the underlying leasehold interest to The Prince's Trust, he has offered a further guarantee. As Reynolds says, "We resisted the bag-of-cash pressure to sell out by means of a long-term interest and kept away from investors and grant givers." This means that the so-called meanwhile use can be a long-term contributor to the economic life of the city. It remains to take the creative solution that Reynolds and Urban Space Management have derived and make it into regular practice so that a wider application of the approach is not dependent on unique urban heroes like Eric Reynolds.

Reynolds himself argues that small-developer entrepreneurs need not be heroes—if the project is approached with a long-term strategy in place:

> If the project is thought through to its natural end at the outset, the stability and growth for the pioneers either on-site or in an alternative location can and should be able to be protected. We try to have an exit strategy in place which we can share with the SME [small or medium enterprises] when they take space. We didn't lose a single stall holder at Camden Lock when we built the Market Hall over the original market yard.

I asked Reynolds if he thought the opportunities for such projects were disappearing with the emergence of London as a place for rampant property speculation, with land values escalating year on year. Reynolds firmly rebutted this idea, noting that there are many parcels of public land sitting unused or underused and that these represent opportunities for markets, for arts-based regeneration, or for small business. It's a question of policy, and Reynolds believes the government should forbid or at the least discourage disposal of government property. He feels that the public sector should "arrange to have more similar opportunities to experiment. Explain the process and means of measurement to the other side: the planners, landowners, and the development professionals. The risk is low because if the attempt fails the land value remains."

The 2016 election of Sadiq Khan as mayor of London has offered some promise in this regard, in the face of continued pressure in the form of higher rents in areas of the city that are improving. Deputy Mayor for Culture Justine Simon has called for "creative enterprise zones." In an interview with the *Evening Standard* in September 2016, she said, "What we want to create is an area where creative people can put down roots and that would be a creative enterprise zone. That's working with local authorities, developers with the creative community, and residents. It's putting a spotlight and a ring around an area."

Mayor Khan followed this up with a competition among the London boroughs for £500,000 (approximately US$615,000) in grants to these creative enterprise zones. The eleven boroughs selected in March 2017 are called upon to focus on securing affordable work and live-work space for the arts, finding support for building enterprise and marketing skills, creating local plan policies that help creative enterprises, and linking the arts with disadvantaged communities. While a pilot project that preceded these grants showed an increase in arts activities, it remains to be seen if an approach centered upon local government will truly foster creative activity.

Deputy Mayor Simon could do worse than take some advice from Eric Reynolds, and so could all mayors concerned about encouraging diversity and the creative economy in their cities.

Trinity Buoy Wharf is a platform upon which the arts can thrive, underpinned by an entrepreneur and a legal arrangement based on use value to the city rather than capital value of the land. What really needs to happen is to make such arrangements possible and to recognize the economic and cultural benefit to the city offered by Trinity Buoy Wharf and Camden and the rest. This will mean that government property mavens will have to accept that there is broader economic value to their surplus land than can be realized by selling it off at highest price. As Reynolds notes, hanging onto the property for the long term and leasing it may result in lower receipts in the short term but much larger benefits in the long term.

After all, look how much richer and livelier a place London is with permanent "meanwhile" uses like Camden Market, Portobello Road, Spitalfields, and now Trinity Buoy Wharf.

Chapter 7

Making Spaces
for the Arts

THE AUTUMN 2016 FIRE in an Oakland warehouse live-work space called the Ghost Ship killed thirty-six young artists and concertgoers and illuminated the fact that many people in successful metropolitan areas were living in substandard accommodation. The Ghost Ship's owner had been cited regularly for safety violations, had made lots of decorative yet flammable wooden modifications, blocked passageways, and provided inadequate exits for the building to be used as a large-group assembly space. At the same time, the building was both meeting a housing need and serving a cultural purpose in a metropolitan area where housing has become prohibitively expensive for many and rents are unaffordable for out-of-the-mainstream cultural events.

The Ghost Ship disaster brought back powerful memories of times in my twenties when I visited friends or attended performances in such spaces in both San Francisco and the East Bay. Cities were still somewhat terra incognita back then. Rents were cheap, and one could survive on the margins by renting vacant storefronts and eating and drinking in dive bars and cafés while pursuing a prolonged education, starting a band, or becoming an artist. I remember amazing pyrotechnic performances by Survival Research Laboratories where it was a surprise when nobody was hurt, as well as overcrowded gigs in lofts and arts studios in abandoned buildings.

Such creative, DIY uses have largely been driven out of San Francisco and Manhattan by now, and they have become rarer in downtown Oakland and Brooklyn. (Chapter 3 explores more fully the value of slack to support creative and entrepreneurial activity.) But they persist, with one official noting that twenty to fifty such warehouse spaces still exist in Oakland, often adjacent to start-up businesses inhabiting similar unregulated premises. Such start-ups are a wellspring of the

Desolate warehouses waiting to become artists' lofts, Brooklyn, NY.
(Credit: "Franklin Artist Lofts, Prospect Heights, Brooklyn, NY" by
Glenn Erikson PhD AIA is licensed under CC BY-ND 4.0.)

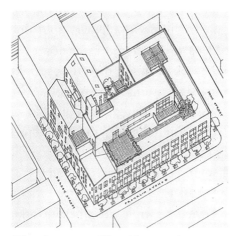

Plan for reuse of Brooklyn warehouses as Franklin Artist Lofts. (Credit: "Franklin Artist Lofts, Prospect Heights, Brooklyn, NY" by Glenn Erikson PhD AIA is licensed under CC BY-ND 4.0.)

business economy, as most jobs are created in growing small businesses.

In the wake of the Ghost Ship disaster, there were crackdowns on DIY spaces for the arts in cities around the country. Building and fire officials responded by shutting down venues, issuing orders to bring properties into compliance with codes, and generally trying to ensure that tragedies don't happen on their watch. This is an expected response to such a terrible event and to the real possibility that local officials will be blamed if other similar tragedies happen.

According to *Billboard* magazine, "Event spaces in Philadelphia, Dallas, Nashville, Indianapolis, and New Haven have reportedly been under greater scrutiny and could face closure. Earlier this week, residents of Baltimore's Bell Foundry art space were evicted for alleged safety violations."[1] A Denver DIY space called Rhinoceropolis was shut down after the Denver Fire Department found extension cords instead of real wiring and a lack of smoke detectors, sprinklers, and residential permits. The ensuing outcry led the City of Denver to convene a meeting to address ways of addressing both the pressing safety issues and the need to find and preserve affordable spaces for the arts.[2]

After initial enforcement actions on some spaces, Oakland mayor Libby Schaff issued an executive order instituting a moratorium on evictions while city officials worked with landlords to bring buildings into compliance, along with other actions to provide technical assistance to building owners. Executive Order 2017-1 states, "We as a City affirm that having housing, workspaces, and cultural gathering spaces in unpermitted spaces that operate safely and responsibly are valuable to the community, and the City should take actions to preserve and legalize these spaces to avoid adverse impacts on the City's affordable housing stock and availability of workspaces and performance venues for vulnerable members of our community."[3]

The music and arts communities have themselves responded by banding together to provide technical assistance and support to venues, studios, and live-work spaces. For example, a group of artists and architects led by a designer named S. Surface crowdsourced a document called "Harm Reduction for DIY Venues: Do It Yourself, Do It Now," with a catalog of sensible actions to take with regard to fire safety and crowd management.[4]

Noting that it is in the interest of mainstream arts institutions like museums to foster DIY spaces, *Smithsonian* magazine published guidance on ways that they could help respond to the impending crackdown, including education on best practices, collaboration, event attendance, paying artists so they can afford to come into compliance, and connecting artists with resources and contacts.[5]

After the December eviction of artists from Baltimore's Bell Foundry, Mayor Catherine Pugh created a task force for making arts spaces safer, with participation from the DIY arts community alongside city officials and arts administrators.[6] The task force seemed focused on the creation of more formal affordable housing for artists, using grants and subsidies in a model similar to that employed by Artspace, a national non-profit that repurposes buildings for artists by using affordable-housing tax credits, historic preservation tax credits, and foundation grants. In addition, the City of Baltimore worked with four existing buildings and a team of pro bono architects and engineers to bring these buildings into compliance. A discussion on improving fire safety in existing spaces revealed the tension between occupants, who wish to make the improvements before engaging with fire officials (for fear of immediate action to shutter spaces), and the fire department, who wish to be involved from the outset.

This demonstrates that arts uses and many start-ups in the creative, small manufacturing, or service sectors are part of the informal economy, existing outside of regulation in a kind of gray zone. Some estimate that as much as 5–10 percent of Gross Domestic Product in developed countries is in the informal sector.[7] Estimates of the amount of informal employment in the United States vary widely, from 3 to 40 percent. While the management of the informal sector as a whole is a huge task, harnessing this energy for urban revitalization and doing so in a way that addresses health and safety needs could form a focused effort.

There is a useful literature on policy approaches to the informal sector both in the developed world and in transitional and developing economies. This literature has come to see the informal economy as a resource and has identified strategies to formalize the informal (gray) sector without driving it out of existence. These can be characterized as regulatory policies—direct control—and indirect policies. Direct-control policies include, on the one hand, stepped-up inspection and enforcement and, on the other, efforts to streamline, simplify, and incentivize informal actors into complying with existing rules and regulations. According to a recent review for the Organization for Economic Cooperation and Development, indirect controls include both education and awareness programs for those in the gray economy and efforts to reform regulatory and taxation regimes to reduce undue burdens on small and informal actors, as well as wider programs to reduce inequities or provide space for informal activities.[8]

With respect to the built environment, both the complexity of regulation and fear of it act as powerful disincentives from coming into conformity, as does a general predilection for Do It Yourself. Compliance with overzealously applied building codes can double the cost of a new building, and the use of the building by an artist or even by a start-up business becomes unaffordable.

While cities are beginning to address the enforcement side of this equation, many are also recognizing the essential role of the arts and the creative sector in their success and are trying new approaches to achieve both goals. For example, New York City's Loft Law, adopted in 1982 and amended in 2013, protects tenants from eviction from nonresidential buildings that were formerly used for manufacturing purposes while providing for public health and safety. Article 7-C of the law defines the buildings and protects the tenants, while article 7-B provides for a process for complying with fire and safety provisions. The steps taken by the municipal governments of Oakland and Baltimore to guarantee safe but affordable live-work space for artists were described above, and the *Washington City Paper* has written of how artists are deserting the gentrification of Washington, DC, for a more supportive home in Baltimore.

London, too, has seen the necessity of protecting the arts as a vital part of its economic appeal, especially in the face of rapidly escalating prices for and increasing offshore investment in property. As was described in chapter 5, London has both a deputy mayor for culture and creative industries and the newly created post of "Night Czar," specifically charged with protecting the nighttime economy. London Mayor Sadiq Khan appointed Amy Lamé—a British American writer, performer, and journalist—as London's first Night Czar in 2016 after the closure of Fabric, an iconic venue, in part to preserve and protect such venues from speculative purchase and redevelopment.

Recognizing the threat to London's artist spaces from such redevelopment, Deputy Mayor Justine Simons has floated the idea of creating "artists' zones" and helping individual artists and organizations to own their own spaces. With a grant of £250,000 (approximately US$310,000) from the mayor, the London Borough of Barking has proposed to become the first Artist Enterprise Zone, already providing studio and office space and supporting cultural venues. The proposal aims to promote Barking as a place for the arts by requiring developers building in the area to provide affordable living and working space for artists.[9]

While this proposal is a step forward, these kinds of solutions don't address the informal side of the equation, instead using formal process to provide subsidized space for artists in high-spec buildings. All too often, such efforts to attract and retain the so-called creative sector miss the target by imposing a top-down vision rather than supporting the DIY spirit that is part of what inspires creatives. A key component of Britain's New Labour push to revitalize former industrial towns and city areas was the funding of museums and arts centers, alongside aspirational master plans. One such, by the architect Will Alsop, envisioned the gritty northern town of Barnsley as a Tuscan hill town modeled on the walled city of Lucca, an idea probably conceived after consuming a few too many bottles of the fine red wines that come from that region. This was supposed to spark a renaissance, but Alsop's vision was never realized, and the flocking of artists to Barnsley was nonexistent.

Will Alsop also was responsible for designing the Tony Blair–era Arts Council's most conspicuous failure: The Public, an arts center in the Black Country. This building was to spearhead the ambitious regeneration of the area, and Alsop's intentionally iconic design ballooned in cost from £57 million to £72 million during construction. But the so-called arts center failed to attract either an arts community or an arts audience, and its annual operating costs exceeded available subsidies. In a ludicrous and sad effort to boost numbers, the local authority counted people coming inside to use the toilets as visitors. Ultimately, it proved too expensive to operate and maintain at a weekly cost of £30,000, and the building was closed permanently by its owner, Sandwell District Council, in 2013. Architects were then retained to convert it into a school.

While Will Alsop was the poster child for some of the Tony Blair–New Labour era's greatest flops, he was really only guilty of taking commissions and designing like a star architect. The real problem was the notion that government could figure out how to make "Cool Britannia" more than a marketing platform. Time and time again, planning strategies for the arts or start-ups were largely composed of more or less equal parts wishful thinking, naff design,[10] and overpriced space that wasn't rough-and-ready for arts or crafts use. From the Millennium Dome's costly failure to the silly attempt to hijack the renaissance of Shoreditch as Tech City, successive governments proved that they couldn't simulate the organic revival of a city neighborhood by young people, artists, and small businesses with conventional procurement, big corporations, and coffee shops.

This doesn't mean that government policy is irrelevant here, as there are ways to better accommodate informal uses in our cities. This is where our old friend, the notion of slack in the built environment (see chapter 5), comes into play. One approach might be to target areas where artists and other actors in the informal economy might be attracted. Often these are former industrial areas near railyards, warehouses, or distribution centers, close to city and town centers and possessing both character and cheap land.

This strategy would aim both to simplify procedures for compliance and rules for occupancy and also to provide tools for occupants and prospective developers seeking to create artists' and creative economy spaces in new or existing repurposed buildings. Zones for the arts and other creative and start-up businesses could offer a variety of opportunities for organic bottom-up enterprise, as opposed to spaces provided by conventional developers through planning obligations and subsidies. An artist enterprise zone might create a platform that allows small-scale arts and maker enterprises to flower and thrive by reducing barriers to entry, providing low-cost space that is protected from speculation through ownership by a trust or charity, and enabling the supportive activities—cafés, galleries, nonchain retail—that attract customers for the arts.

Clearly Trinity Buoy Wharf is an example of this approach, as is the major effort at Folkestone on the South Coast, generously funded by Sir Roger De Haan. At Folkestone the early emphasis was on rehabbing storefronts and the spaces upstairs for artists' galleries, studios, and living spaces and renting them affordably. Over time, as a local artist community emerged, a program of events, exhibitions, and artist residencies and workshops was introduced. After some years of that, a new arts venue was built, reversing the usual course of these schemes by supporting the artists rather than hoping that an iconic building will work magic.

A city that wants to attract or retain artists and makers could reduce the complexity and cost of getting buildings permitted by focusing on life safety issues, demystifying them, and creating an amnesty for existing uses, so long as they are brought into compliance. This would mean identifying facilitators who have the political support to keep artists in place, albeit safely.

It should be possible to build new studio spaces for artists in addition to reoccupying and reusing old warehouses and lofts. A city could commission the development of designs for small-scale, low-cost, bare-bones studio, loft, and workshop building types, as well as single-room-occupancy building types, and get them preapproved.

Affordability and accessibility for start-ups and artists can be preserved through a variety of means, including restricting land assembly within the zone and prohibiting the provision of large-floor-plate retail. In addition, assistance could be provided to help with the creation of lean ownership models such as community land trusts or cooperatives to preserve affordability. At the same time, it would be important to provide for densification and multifamily housing close to but not in the "Pink Zone"—an area within the city where red tape is lightened to facilitate redevelopment.

There is a need for guidance for using the existing building code for lofts, studios, and music and performance venues, drawing on case studies of work-arounds by people doing these kinds of projects on a limited budget rather than with extensive grant subsidies, which will always lead to more complex and expensive solutions.

Ideally, a zone for the creative economy would be located in a part of the city that is not already experiencing gentrification and speculation in land and buildings, with vacant or underutilized commercial, warehouse, or manufacturing buildings or parcels, and reasonable accessibility. The classic district for the arts has been the old warehouse and loft areas of industrial cities, such as Shoreditch in London or SoHo and TriBeCa in New York. The arts can thrive just as well in a reuse of the midcentury highway strip, repurposing auto dealerships, drive-up storefronts, service stations and garages, and older public buildings.

Chapter 8

Filling in the Missing Pieces: Lean Urbanism

with Brian Falk

Austin in the 1970s, Vancouver's Granville Island, London's Trinity Buoy Wharf, Rose Town in Jamaica, and on a very different scale, the city of Detroit all have one big thing in common: they show how individuals in communities have been able to find the empty or underutilized spaces in cities and transform them into more housing, places for commerce or other kinds of enterprise, and spaces for learning and making art. Why aren't more people building their communities themselves? The reasons are many, but the most obvious is that it is so difficult. Since World War II, a thicket of public-sector regulations and private-sector financial requirements have grown up around neighborhood zoning, parking requirements, and rehabilitating older structures. Virtually every aspect of these systems that govern urban development privileges the big projects and burdens the small ones. And it makes it harder for disinvested communities and cities to rebuild from the ground up.

In 2013, architect and urban designer Andrés Duany began talking about the need to make community-building easier and less expensive. What were needed were simpler, more basic types of architecture, urban design, and development and simpler processes for approving the design and construction of projects. Development, Duany explained, had become too difficult, too time-consuming, and too expensive. The processes were challenging for all projects, but especially so for smaller and one-off projects, and often weren't accessible at all to individuals and small entrepreneurs.

To level the playing field, Duany proposed the creation of a sort of toolkit to make community-building less onerous. He called it Lean Urbanism. It draws on the insights of New Urbanism but aims to fill a gap in terms of allowing neighborhood- and city-building at a smaller scale. Lean Urbanism is an approach to community-building that requires fewer resources. It's a response to the requirements, complexities, and costs that disproportionately burden small-scale developers, builders, and entrepreneurs. It facilitates a return to mixed-use, walkable, and contextual communities, and it makes it easier to take advantage of spatial slack, fill in the empty spaces, and complete a neighborhood.

Duany compared the barriers that face would-be developers today to the situation when he and his business partner and wife, Elizabeth Plater-Zyberk, designed the traditional coastal town of Seaside, Florida, in the late 1970s. Because the land was privately owned and unincorporated, there was no need to ask a zoning department for development approval or for a building department to approve the house plans or inspect the cottages as they were built. The homes in Seaside were designed following vernacular architecture and built using vernacular materials. In Florida, this meant metal roofs that could survive storms, overhanging eaves that shaded the windows and walls from the heat of the sun, and elevated floors that would allow the air and water to flow beneath the buildings. These vernacular designs and materials were also inexpensive, as was the approach to infrastructure. For example, using pavers instead of asphalt and gravel instead of concrete allowed the developer to provide it only where houses were being built and wait for new ones before providing more.

Today there are planning and building departments in nearly every city, town, and county in the United States. Duany now anticipates that when he designs a new community, the developers will work for years to obtain approval to build it. The zoning codes that those planning departments administer

Homes in pedestrian-oriented Seaside, Florida, in 1986. (Credit: State Archives of Florida, Florida Memory.)

regulate in great detail the way land can be developed and used. The code that governed Seaside was written on a single page, but today most codes are so long and complex that few people read them. Even the staff who administer them might be unaware of some of their requirements, and often they're also unfamiliar with some of the things the codes allow. If developers have deep enough pockets, or if the projects are big enough to justify the cost, they hire specialists to guide them through the approvals process, like Sherpas in the Himalayas. Yet even with these guides, and with "fixers" hired to solve the regulatory and bureaucratic problems that inevitably arise, the approval process takes time that must be amortized in the project budget.

Beginning in the 1950s, it became common for zoning codes to be rewritten to encourage the kind of suburban development that was prominent in many areas. New minimum requirements were added for lot and building sizes, setbacks from the lot lines, and off-street parking. And of course these zoning codes restricted the types of uses allowed on the land. Commercial activities were prohibited in residential areas, and multifamily homes were prohibited in single-family areas. For example, in a neighborhood of Dallas called Oak Cliff, sometime in the 1940s it became illegal to put flowers outside a building, hang an awning, or put café seating or display goods on the sidewalk. In effect, anything that encouraged public street life was illegal and would incur a stiff fine.

As the codes were rewritten, they were often applied to entire municipalities, despite the fact that the existing buildings and communities might not conform to the new requirements. Houses on lots that were too small or that didn't have enough off-street parking according to the new code couldn't be substantially renovated or redeveloped. A homeowner wanting to convert a garage into an apartment for an elderly grandmother wasn't allowed to do it. Or if the homeowner were an elderly grandmother who needed to downsize and wanted to convert her garage into an apartment for herself, rent out her home to provide income, and stay in her neighborhood, she wasn't permitted to do so. Doubling up or taking in boarders, a common practice in earlier periods that was revived and encouraged during World War II (see chapter 4), wasn't allowed in single-family zones. And of course single-family homes couldn't be replaced with multifamily buildings, even if that was the predominant character of the neighborhood.

Commercial properties faced similar restrictions. Corner stores and offices were no longer permitted in residential areas, and in the neighborhood main streets and downtowns, new minimum requirements for off-street parking made new construction, and sometimes even renovation, impossible. The

Garage repurposed into accessory live-work unit, Austin, TX.
(Credit: courtesy of Sarah Campbell.)

result was that vast swaths of cities and towns were rendered "nonconforming," left in legal limbo. With renovation and new construction effectively prohibited, many of those areas stagnated and then declined.

Johnny Sanphillippo is a blogger, architecture enthusiast, and occasional small-scale developer who recounted the story of his attempt to purchase and rehab an abandoned house in Cincinnati. After five years of exploring the city, he decided that the Northside neighborhood felt like home and he wanted to be a part of its reinvention. On a street where a third of the homes were abandoned, he bought a small house at a low price. He hired a design-build firm to add a second story to the home, matching the existing buildings on either side and creating two apartments to rent. But the zoning code forbade new construction or renovation to create duplexes, despite the original multifamily character of the neighborhood.

Sanphillippo went back to the drawing board. He asked his designer to create new plans, this time for a two-story, single-family home. But according to the zoning code, the lot was too small for any home, and the existing structure didn't conform to the setback and other requirements. The original building was grandfathered, but adding a second story would render it out of compliance. The only option the code allowed was to renovate the existing single-story building, but the likely rental income didn't justify the expense.

Sanphillippo and the designer then asked the City to give them a variance from the code, at which point they entered the arcane, time-consuming, and frustrating process of requesting approval. A year later, after the required variance hearings (and the waiting) and the required review board meetings (and more waiting) plus a few thousand dollars paid to the designer, they had gotten nowhere. Sanphillippo gave up the fight and sold the property. Yet, in that same time frame, a 130-unit apartment complex was approved and built just three blocks away.[1]

Perhaps the approvals process made it easier to obtain permits for a project that size, or perhaps the city deemed the larger project a "catalyst" for neighborhood revitalization and helped remove the obstacles to development, or maybe the larger project's budget justified the expense of a code Sherpa or a fixer. Whatever the reason, Sanphillippo's experience offers an example of how existing regulations create relative privilege for large projects and burden small-scale entrepreneurs. It should not be more difficult to get approval for two units than for 130.

Building codes are ubiquitous, too. The codes were created with noble intentions such as avoiding tenement conditions and improving substandard housing. By and large they've been successful in improving public safety, but those successes also have brought a number of unintended consequences. One is that renovating buildings often becomes prohibitively difficult and expensive. Stairs that met the code requirements when they were built are too narrow or too steep to meet the current requirements that are triggered by renovation, even though they may be structurally sound. Or stairs and egresses must be added to get approval for a renovation, though they wouldn't be required if the building were not being renovated. Those added costs and complexities kill many small projects.

Another frequent upgrade requirement is electrical wiring. Renovation may trigger a requirement to install updated wiring, and if the existing conduits in the walls are too narrow to hold the thicker new wiring, the conduits have to be replaced, too, which means walls have to be torn apart and then repaired. If the renovation is a small project, such as a single apartment or commercial space in a multistory building, that conduit will probably also have to be replaced in the floors above and below, increasing the difficulty and expense to the point that the renovation might not be justified. This often causes older buildings to deteriorate until they can be purchased whole at a low price and renovated all at once or demolished and replaced altogether.

Building codes were once tailored for regional building materials and methods, but they have now become standardized, with the same codes applied to cities and towns across the country, meaning that vernacular designs and materials like those used in Seaside may be prohibited or too difficult to use, despite their lower costs and advantages for local climates. Two houses built by their owners just outside Austin, Texas, offer concrete examples of successful lean and green uses of unconventional building materials. One has rammed earth walls—a mixture of sand, gravel, and clay tamped into a mold—which are extremely energy-efficient both to build and to operate, staying cool even in Texas's one-hundred-plus-degree summers. The other is insulated with straw bales within the walls, which also offers cost-effective natural insulation. Austin's building code had supported green building measures such as straw-bale construction since 2000. Yet despite the advantages of their readily available construction materials, low cost, and natural climate adaptability, both of these houses would have had a hard time getting financing and insurance. Yet both offer obvious answers to the challenges of making housing affordable in an overheated (in both senses of the word) housing market like Austin's. As with zoning codes, building codes and lender requirements present hurdles if the construction is the least bit unusual. Administrators who are unfamiliar with the allowances in the code or with the vernacular materials and techniques may not even realize they could lawfully permit their use. And if a lender or insurance broker faces unusual construction, they may not understand how to describe it or may require a professional engineer's stamp of approval. If the project is big enough, the negotiation and the wait might be justified, but that's less likely for small projects.

In addition to the challenge of required building improvements, expansion or new construction sometimes requires that infrastructure be provided or improved. Those infrastructure improvements could be minor, such as new sidewalks or landscaping, or major, such as installing a larger water main in the street in front of the building. These costs might be absorbed by a larger project but they can kill a smaller one. And like the straw-bale home, lean green infrastructure such as bioswales to capture rainwater, rather than expensive new storm sewers, can make sense but have difficulty getting permits.

Given these examples, it's easy to see the discouraging effects that such requirements can have on small individual projects. But what might not be so easy to see are the effects they have on entire communities. When small-scale, incremental development—of buildings or businesses—isn't possible, fewer members of a community can participate in community-building and revitalization. Affordable upgrades to existing buildings may be beyond the reach of local residents. Big projects are usually owned by investors from outside the community. They might create some local jobs, but most of the income and wealth generated by big projects leave the community. Big projects also mean big changes for communities.

Some are positive and some are not, but when members of the community can't participate in the economic development, they have less influence over how their community evolves.

Understanding this dynamic is important both for communities where the market is hot and for those that are economically depressed. In areas where development interest is high, small projects and incremental growth can help moderate the speed and character of change and allow community members to not only avoid displacement but even benefit from the revitalization. As urban futurist Stewart Brand has said, "Tweaking the system is, I think, not only the most efficient way to make the system go in interesting ways . . . but also the safest way."[2]

Facilitating smaller-scale, more locally driven projects is also important for communities that need revitalization. Big projects are unlikely to be proposed in such communities unless they're enticed with subsidies such as tax abatements or public-private partnerships. When small projects are feasible, they allow community members to participate in the revitalization, building wealth in the community and allowing them—whether individually or in groups such as arts collectives—to determine the neighborhood's character. But this happens only when the financial, regulatory, and bureaucratic barriers are low.

What do lean—locally driven, small-scale, and sustainable—projects look like? Detroit offers some examples. Like many Rust Belt cities, Detroit suffered from deindustrialization and the flight of middle-class, generally white, residents to surrounding suburbs in the 1950s and '60s. By some estimates, more than half of the residential lots in the city were abandoned. After decades of decline, the city government went bankrupt. With limited resources, the City struggled to provide municipal services. While that caused many difficulties for residents, there was a silver lining: properties could be bought at low cost, and less governmental oversight reduced the cost to renovate them. That allowed creativity and entrepreneurial spirit to generate some exciting examples of revitalization in neighborhoods and communities, including vibrant arts cooperatives, small-scale businesses, and homes.

The Power House, a local enterprise that generates electricity through solar and wind power, is working to become an off-the-grid electric-power generator and distributor and is helping to revive and repurpose a neighborhood of live and work spaces through adaptive reuse. Back Alley Bikes began as a summer program where neighborhood kids could learn bike repair and possibly earn bikes of their own. It has developed a retail bike shop, and the Motor City has been creating bike lanes in streets throughout the city to encourage bicycling as an alternative form of transportation.[3]

When Andrés Duany, Hank Dittmar, and Brian Falk formed the Project for Lean Urbanism, with the support of the John S. and James L. Knight Foundation, Detroit served as an early inspiration.

The project began with research to identify problems and propose solutions.[4] They then began a series of pilot projects to test solutions, develop tools for "Making Small Possible," and make those tools widely available, spreading the knowledge from the professionals to the community builders and entrepreneurs. The final goal is to release a kit of tools that are free for anyone to use and to raise awareness of the value of small-scale, incremental development and the need for a level playing field.[5]

For the pilot projects, they looked for communities with municipal leadership that supported reducing process burdens for small enterprise, development, self-building, and retrofit; support among local businesses, residents, and organizations; and empty lots, vacant buildings, and older neighborhoods that could be seen as assets rather than liabilities. The primary tool developed in the pilot projects is what they call a Pink Zone—an area within the city where red tape is lightened to facilitate redevelopment.

Savannah, where Hank Dittmar reported that he found kindred spirits who wanted to revitalize the city's more blighted areas without sacrificing its historic fabric, is a great place to test the Lean Urbanist approach, and it was chosen for a pilot project. The city begins with a famously beautiful layout, designed by James Oglethorpe in the colonial era, around a series of squares surrounded by housing, ensuring public open space. The project began with a "Lean Scan" that identified common barriers to small projects and two potential areas for Pink Zones. The Lean Scan was followed by a workshop to meet with small developers, businesspeople, and city staff to agree on new protocols to enable redevelopment in the Pink Zone without endangering public safety.

Kevin Klinkenberg, who ran the nonprofit partner organization that submitted the application for Savannah to become a Lean Urbanism pilot, recalls that the project encountered delays when a new mayor and city council came on board, along with a new city manager who made substantial changes to city government, and the City rewrote its entire zoning code, pushing back its consideration of creating Pink Zones. Now Savannah faces another municipal election.[6] The project also has encountered predictable challenges: "Anytime you try to engage a city and get it to do less, that will be a challenging conversation because the nature of bureaucracies is to grow.

[And] behind every rule and ordinance and code there is a reason and a good intention, but the accumulation of those things makes it hard to do anything."[7]

Productive conversations about how government can provide platforms for success, and many individuals within city government who understand and value the Lean Urbanist approach of supporting small business and small conversions of existing spaces, make the participants confident that the Pink Zone will happen, if not on their original time frame. On the progress side, the workshop identified a way to use city-owned land to host an occasional market, and that is happening.

Such a method of development is informed by the demonstration projects of Tactical Urbanism and Better Block, which take a "quick-build" approach to demonstrating how an underutilized place could be different. For example, community members may band together to create temporary bike lanes or pedestrian crossings with brightly colored tape, a pop-up sidewalk "parkette" with a few benches and potted plants, or a sidewalk art gallery. The point is to get community members to experience—and ideally to help create—a different way of using their public space and to inspire them to make such changes permanent. It is also inspired by the "meanwhile" uses of England (as was described in chapter 6).

In areas where real estate development isn't yet justified by the market, property owners often feel that they need to wait until the market improves. Their vacant properties, though, often hinder that improvement. But rather than doing nothing until they can complete their ideal projects, there are things they can do in the meantime. For example, they might envision retail buildings for their property on the neighborhood's main street, but in the meantime they could begin with inexpensive temporary buildings on the site or even with tents and tables. They might envision restaurants on their property, but in the meantime they could begin with food trucks. Inspired by Reynolds, Lean Urbanism also calls this approach "meantime uses." In a way similar to how Tactical Urbanism or Better Block projects can prove concepts and demonstrate changes to the public realm, these meantime uses can be a less expensive, easier, faster way to use private properties, improve the market, and recruit and train entrepreneurs and developers from the local community.

The projects can take any number of forms on a spectrum of development, from the most humble and temporary on one end to the most sophisticated and permanent on the other. The form is determined by what is feasible at the time, and when the market justifies further investment, the form can be replaced by something more sophisticated and permanent. Meantime uses can be employed on a single property, but they're more powerful when combined and coordinated among multiple neighboring properties. This idea was proposed in another pilot project in Lafayette, Louisiana, where the Pink Zone includes a commercial corridor that was once a neighborhood main street but is today lined with many empty lots.

Meantime uses are particularly useful in Pink Zones where revitalization is a goal, but they can also provide a way for locals to participate in and benefit from a hotter market. They're vulnerable, however, to the same regulatory and bureaucratic obstacles as other small-scale projects, so changes to zoning or temporary-use permits may be needed to allow them.

The results of Lean Projects include community members who have been enabled and trained to shape their communities, codes, and processes that level the playing field for small-scale economic development, and tools and techniques that can be replicated in other communities.

By "Making Small Possible," Lean Urbanism offers a return to the way we built cities before excessive regulations: one or two houses, retail shops, and workshops at a time. It is incremental, modest development by small-scale builders and developers that can provide affordability without subsidies. It is economic development that focuses on the Main Street businesses that provide benefits to the local community. It is a way for a community to revitalize itself while preserving local character and benefiting local residents. The creation of Pink Zones is a way to formalize, encourage, and support this DIY version of the American Dream.

Some might argue that Making Small Possible is antithetical to the widespread change needed to meet the massive problems of concentrated poverty and neighborhood decline. But Making Small Possible can be implemented on a large scale. It is only a matter of creating platforms that support a large number of small, incremental improvements.

What's more, the gradual approach and sensitive knitting-together of community resources supports the goal of increasing local home and business ownership and the revitalization and stability that they bring to a community. In many communities, we find that small, funky workspaces are fully occupied. These small business spaces are the backbone of the economy, yet we don't focus on making more of them.

Lean Urbanism is thus a tool not only for a simpler and more cost-effective scale of revitalization but also for one that is aimed at ensuring community benefit and control of the process—developing the social capital of a community along with the built capital. It's a tool for taking advantage of the slack in cities and encouraging DIY community-building.

Chapter 9

Too Small to Matter? The Persistence of the Informal

I HAVE LEFT THE MOST OBVIOUS OBJECTIONS to my thesis until the end. I think there are two main arguments against the DIY City.

The first objection I keep hearing is that enduring shibboleth of what the American writer and activist Rebecca Solnit calls the "miserable Left": "this approach is a compromise and like all compromises should be abjured." That is, only by holding out for the complete collapse of the neoliberal consensus can meaningful change be achieved, and support of small enterprise and shopkeepers and nonprofits is only a halfway measure. To which I can only respond that I am choosing to live in the world we have and not the one I wish we had.

The second argument is more cogent. It goes like this: "Isn't small too small to matter? Aren't the emergent corporate monopolies and cartels so vast as to render DIY irrelevant?" Stewart Brand's original insight for the *Whole Earth Catalog* is entirely relevant here. He argued that both hippie utopianism and the structural critique made by the New Left in the sixties were dependent on either changes to human nature or magical thinking, and that tweaking the system was much more likely to change things. Like the *Whole Earth Catalog*, the Lean Urbanism and incremental development movements are about providing people with access to tools and people then using those tools to exploit gaps in a system that is engineered for large organizations and large numbers.

A further answer to the "too small to matter" objection requires a diversion from the developed economies we have mostly been looking at to look at trends in the developing world, to slums, and to the informal, or gray, economy.

Slums are often seen as an embarrassment, as a failure of society to provide for the poor, and as a challenge to the orderly provision of housing and jobs. The first impulse in many countries has been to knock them down, repossess the land for urban development, and transfer it, along with land titles, to well-connected, conventionally financed developers. This kind of urban removal has been resisted by squatters whenever and wherever tried, often successfully.

The problems with slums have been well documented, but they bear repeating briefly: crime, poor sanitation, lack of potable water, lack of secure tenure, lack of public space, and flimsy, overcrowded dwellings. Despite significant progress in improving living conditions over the past fifteen years,

> in our world, one in eight people live in slums. In total, around a billion people live in slum conditions today. . . . In spite of great progress in improving slums and preventing their formation—represented by a decrease from 39 percent to 30 percent of urban population living in slums in developing

countries between 2000 and 2014—absolute numbers continue to grow, and the slum challenge remains a critical factor for the persistence of poverty in the world.[1]

Resistance to these conditions and to relocation policies led to the slum dwellers' movement, whereby people living in shacks and slums have advocated for secure tenure, official postal addresses, infrastructure, and sanitation and have organized themselves to improve living conditions. The exemplar for this approach is the Mumbai slum of Dharavi, where Jockin Arputham, founder of the slum dwellers' movement and Slum/Shack Dwellers International, organized the community's women to provide toilets and worked to resist the forced removal of people from the city's largest slum.

I met Mr. Arputham in 2009, when The Prince's Foundation's annual conference was titled "Globalisation from the Bottom Up." I invited him, along with Michael Black from Rose Town, Jamaica, to speak at a conference of international figures keynoted by Prince Charles. Arputham told the story of persistent government efforts to remove the settlers from Dharavi and the resistance that lead to the formation of the slum dwellers' movement. Over many years an uneasy truce seemed to have been arrived at, and the slum dwellers moved from organizing to resist to organizing to improve. In each quarter of the slum, the women began to collect funds for the installation of toilets, holding back a small sum from the family wage packet to contribute to a communal kitty. A family was appointed guardian of the toilet, tasked with keeping it clean and with collecting the pittance contributed each time it was used.

The audience of international bigwigs was nonplussed to hear about building toilets rather than explanations of aid policy, but as Arputham went on, the titters ceased and people began to pick up on his energy and passion. Michael Black from Jamaica followed. He talked not about housing models or finance structures, but about asking the mothers and grandmothers from both sides of the gang-torn Trench Town neighborhood to come together to walk in a show of unity and reconnection. The point they made was clear: people had the power to make change themselves, and governments and aid agencies too often overlook—or worse, destroy through relocation—the social capital that exists in the poorest communities.

Slums persist, despite government efforts to destroy them or relocate their residents, because of the existence and resilience of these social and economic networks and the continuation of loose and close ties and affiliations, as well as the lack of alternative places to live and work. Relocation is resisted because it disrupts these useful networks. Like the settlement houses in nineteenth-century Chicago slums or their Victorian equivalents in England, slums are places with formal and informal social services that poor people entering the city use and rely on.

Moreover, slums often replicate age-old, planetwide urban patterns of village, town, and city life. Importantly, slums tend to create versions of the lively, mixed-use street that predates the superblock and the wide arterial road.

There are useful patterns for the future in the social and physical organization of slums, as HRH The Prince of Wales said in a 2009 speech that concluded the Globalisation from the Bottom Up conference:

> Indeed, whenever I have visited informal settlements such as, for example, Dharavi in Mumbai in 2003, I find an underlying, intuitive "grammar of design" that subconsciously produces somewhere that is walkable, mixed-use, and adapted to local

climate and materials, which is totally absent from the faceless slab blocks that are still being built around the world to "warehouse" the poor.[2]

If one wishes to retain both the social and the physical characteristics of resilient urban form, it becomes imperative to empower local residents, enable them to get more secure land tenure, provide services, and facilitate the gradual improvement of housing, infrastructure, and economy.

Within and outside of informal settlements, a large part of the world participates in the informal economy: working, trading, or living without necessarily asking permission, paying taxes, or following regulations. Estimates on the scale of the informal economy vary widely, but it is enormous. According to UN Habitat, "In many developing countries, informal employment comprises more than half of non-agricultural employment. In low-income countries, informal employment makes up 70–95 percent of total employment (including agriculture) and is found mainly in the informal sector."[3]

The International Labor Office in Geneva has published the most comprehensive survey of informal employment. It found that, for example, informal employment made up over one-third of urban employment in India and a much higher percentage in Africa. The study also found that policies to regulate the informal sector by improving working conditions rather than discouraging it not only could be pro-poor but also could improve gender equality. In all the countries surveyed, the proportion of women working in the informal sector was higher than that of men, partly because of the preponderance of home-based work.

The informal sector, or gray economy, ranges from the tiny catering business serving meals from a home kitchen or the carpenter working for cash, to street vendors reselling goods purchased in markets, to artists and tinkerers living and working in lofts, garages, and storefronts, and to oligarchs and gangsters laundering cash through real estate in cities like London, Vancouver, and Sydney. Most are small businesses skirting the law because the cost or hassle of compliance is perceived to be too great. The gray economy is often untaxed, unregulated, and invisible; it represents both a route out of poverty and a disaster waiting to happen due to such problems as unsanitary kitchens, pit toilets, structurally deficient buildings, and fire safety problems.

By and large, most informal entrepreneurs would like to come into compliance, and for many, in fact, the cost of complying with health and safety provisions is not prohibitive. As we have seen, though, regulation and permitting often go far beyond protecting the public interest in health, safety, and welfare to securing the interests of entrenched industries, suppliers who stake standard-setting bodies, and local cultural lobbies and interest groups.

The drivers for informality in cities come from both above and below. Martha Chen and colleagues define this tension:

The urban poor create informal settlements or pursue informal livelihoods by operating in the gaps in formal rules (de jure and/or de facto) and the gaps in the use of urban space (temporal and/or spatial). Meanwhile, the state both defines the formal rules (who and what is considered legal/illegal or formal/informal) and creates authorized exceptions to them, including the use of public space, often in collusion with powerful vested interests. Put another way, there are exceptions authorized by the state that the elite take advantage of, and unauthorized exceptions that the non-elite create on their own for survival.[4]

Despite a formidable body of regulation and enforcement, the informal economy persists. And this gives me hope, for it represents a real and sustained resistance to the monopolies and oligopolies that are coming to dominate many economic sectors. Alongside the increasing power of a limited number of global conglomerates skirting tax laws and shadowy capital seeking places to land, there exists a third global system in the informal economy of home-based work, street traders, and start-up entrepreneurs, and its persistence and vitality mean that there is a continuing place for the small scale.

The formal and informal economies can come into conflict when urban renewal or large-scale investment plans target slums and other older neighborhoods in the city. As Chen notes, this has had a destructive effect in the developing world:

> Another worrisome trend is the intensification of forced evic-
> tions driven by, among other factors, large-scale urban renewal
> projects, the hosting of mega events, and the recent global
> recession. When slum communities are evicted or relocated,
> home-based producers in those communities temporarily lose
> both their home and their workplace. They are often relocated
> to housing with fewer basic services and to locations at a greater
> distance from markets for raw materials and finished goods or
> from the contractors who sub-contract work to them.[5]

Rather than a development model that imports the structures and legal frameworks of the developed world into the
Global South, albeit with updates such as the "smart city,"
perhaps what is needed is a two-way conversation in which
efforts to improve living conditions and reduce inequality in
developing cities are accompanied with a campaign to bring
the messy life and informality of the small scale into the

developed city. This can be an antidote to the increasing trend toward financialization and discouragement of small enterprise, and perhaps a partial answer to the restructuring of work and the increasing fragility of many people's livelihoods in the twenty-first-century city.

After all, Ela Bhatt, the founder of India's Self-Employed Women's Association, has a prescription for developing cities that seems like a pretty solid response to the problems in our gentrifying cities as outlined in this book:

> The challenge is to convince the policy makers to promote and encourage hybrid economies in which micro-businesses can coexist alongside small, medium, and large businesses: in which the street vendors can coexist alongside the kiosks, retail shops, and large malls. . . . Just as the policy makers encourage biodiversity, they should encourage economic diversity. Also, they should try to promote a level playing field in which all sizes of businesses and all categories of workers can compete on equal and fair terms.[6]

This means promoting small enterprise, rather than discouraging it, by adopting regulations that protect public health and safety while recognizing the smaller harm potential of many small enterprises. It also means comprehensive planning that keeps the small scale in mind, not just the usual default position that favors large-scale development.

More and more, it seems that there is a false choice between bottom-up and top-down, and that DIY can prompt and model the change that is needed, while policy and finance can enable it. Sometimes government should act directly, especially with infrastructure like roads, water, and sewer. However, the compact that is needed is not between multinational contractors and government in so-called public-private partnerships, but between residents and their elected and appointed representatives. It was the actions of activist squatters in the Bengali Housing Action Group, led by Terry Fitzgerald, to open empty public housing at Arnold's Circus in London's Hoxton in the seventies to families from Bangladesh that prompted Greater London Council leader George Tremlett, a Tory, to rethink the council's housing policy and open up and repair their housing stock in consultation with the prospective occupants. The story was well told in the BBC documentary series *The Secret History of Our Streets*.

One of my favorite examples of the way that DIY and informal or unsanctioned action can prompt salutary action by government comes from Vienna, Austria, in the years between the First and Second World Wars. Vienna, like much of Europe after the devastation of the war, faced a severe housing shortage, and the market was not responding. What emerged was called the Wild Settlement movement, an unsanctioned effort by people to build their own housing on garden allotment plots and abandoned railway lands. Little cottages began to appear all over, and the people organized building materials, developed simple house plans, and began making do for themselves.

In those years of social change, some professionals began to take notice. One was the architect Adolf Loos, famed for his adage that "ornament is a crime" and for buildings so beautifully crafted that ornament was integral. Loos and colleagues began to design homes for the Wild Settlers, creating house plans and block plans for their use. This in turn prompted the city authorities to begin to address the housing shortage themselves, and Adolf Loos became the city architect. Over a fifteen-year period, using designs by Loos and others, Vienna built homes for 200,000 people in large midrise courtyard blocks compete with nurseries, schools, shops, and gardens.[7] This period became known as Red Vienna, when a social democratic government put the needs of the residents first. The homes that resulted are still prized, and architects visit Vienna to study the massive Karl Marx-Hof and more moderately sized courtyard projects such as Rabenhof and Am Fuchsenfeld.

The fascist takeover of Austria put a stop to the housing program and to Red Vienna, and conservative national governments after the war have tried to thwart the provision of rental housing as the housing model of choice for Vienna. The city has persisted, however, and today, fully 80 percent of the city's population lives in rental housing stock supplied for both working-class and low-income, non-working-class people, although these people are provided an additional subsidy. As a result, renting a home is the norm, and the percentage of income that the Viennese devote to shelter—no more than 25 percent—is far less than the European average and a fraction of that of Londoners.[8] This creates a kind of slack and a quality of life that is impossible if half of one's income goes to putting a roof over one's head.

Yale anthropology professor James C. Scott argues that positive social change comes not from organized lobby groups or solely from government policy but instead from small acts of resistance by less organized groups and the use of the tactics at hand:

> Elites, controlling the lawmaking machinery of the state, have deployed bills of enclosure, paper titles, and freehold tenure, not to mention the police, gamekeepers, forest guards, the courts, and the gibbet to establish and defend their property rights. Peasants and subaltern groups, having no access to

such heavy weaponry, have instead relied on techniques such as poaching, pilfering, and squatting to contest those claims and assert their own.[9]

Citing the American civil rights movement, Scott notes that efforts to coordinate the mass breaking-out of activism and civil disobedience by established progressive groups failed and that, paradoxically, this forced political institutions to react more comprehensively than if they had been negotiating outcomes. He wonders, though, if change can only come from epochal, extremely disruptive actions that demonstrate viscerally that existing frameworks are inadequate. The Wild Settlers in Red Vienna provide an example of a successful disruption that is nonviolent yet compelling. Interestingly, Scott finds the locus for social change not primarily in the oppressed poor but in the petty bourgeoisie, the small businesspeople, shopkeepers, and smallholders whose desire for autonomy, for a place in the community, is mirrored by the poor. He sees the petty bourgeoisie as the carriers of vernacular culture, the wellspring for land reform and property rights, and a primary source of innovation. Embracing the informal to allow these positives to flower is surely one role for the state.

Maybe this support for the small doesn't rise to the level of a grand theory, and maybe the future inevitably belongs to machines, presided over by big multinational corporations. Somehow, I doubt that a consensus on an alternate future can be reached. My experience over the years has taught me that there may not be one alternate future anyway and that most attempts at a grand theory end up having serious unforeseen consequences or being too damn hard to pull off. Stewart Brand points out, "Tweaking the system is, I think, not only the most efficient way to make the system go in interesting

The Seven Dials intersection and obelisk, London, UK, a favorite location for the author. (Credit: photo by Christopher Woo.)

ways . . . but also the safest way, because when you try to horse the whole system around in a big way, you can get into big horsing-around problems, but if you tweak it, it will adjust to the tweak."[10]

In the end, making small happen is also about many small things: appropriate regulation and oversight that correlates with scale, networks of mutual support, rethinking the role of land in cities, and once again promoting sharing and small business. It's also about recognizing the huge gaps that have appeared in our provision of housing, in our social care, and in our job markets and seeing these as opportunities for us to do it ourselves.

As Leonard Cohen sang in his song "Anthem," "There is a crack in everything—that's how the light gets in." In my experience, the more space we leave for small, the more humans will fill it. Perhaps this is where hope lies.

Notes

Introduction

1. "Chicago, Offering Big Incentives, Will Be Boeing's New Home," *New York Times* (May 11, 2001), https://www.nytimes.com/2001/05/11/business/chicago-offering-big-incentives-will-be-boeing-s-new-home.html.

2. "How the Move Downtown Is Paying Off for McDonald's," *Crain's Chicago Business* (July 30, 2019), https://www.chicagobusiness.com/joe-cahill-business/how-move-downtown-paying-mcdonalds.

Chapter 1

1. Rob Shaw, "B.C. Speculation Tax Figures Show Foreign Owners Hardest Hit as Expected Take Soars," *Vancouver Sun* (July 11, 2019), https://vancouversun.com/news/local-news/early-speculation-tax-figures-show-foreign-owners-hardest-hit.

2. Anthony Perl notes that these observations were made at the peak of speculative buying in Vancouver and that both the city and the province have since enacted taxes on absentee and offshore ownership that have curbed the most speculative excesses. He says, however, that housing is still unaffordable, with many young people largely priced out of Vancouver or even the greater metro area. In his opinion, it would take decades of creating affordable housing to correct the imbalance.—Ed.

3. Mike Hager, "Empty Vancouver Homes Receiving Global Attention with Blog," *Vancouver Sun* (October 7, 2014), http://www.vancouversun.com/business/Empty+Vancouver+homes+receiving+global+attention+with+blog/10223503/story.html.

4. "Millennials Spend Three Times More on Housing than Grandparents," *Guardian* (September 20, 2017), https://www.theguardian.com/society/2017/sep/20/millennials-spend-three-times-more-of-income-on-housing-than-grandparents.

5. Janna Matlack and Jacob Vigdor, "Do Rising Tides Lift All Prices?" NBER Working Paper 12331 (NBER, June 2006), 27, https://www.nber.org/papers/w12331.pdf.

6. Judith Rodin, "Realizing the Resilience Dividend," Rockefeller Foundation (January 22, 2014), https://www.rockefellerfoundation.org/blog/realizing-resilience-dividend/.

Chapter 2

1. League of American Bicyclists, "Using Federal Data for Bicycle Friendly States," https://bikeleague.org/sites/default/files/federal_data_for_bfs.pdf.

2. Stewart Brand, "Pace Layering: How Complex Systems Learn and Keep Learning," *Journal of Design and Science* (January 17, 2018), https://jods.mitpress.mit.edu/pub/issue3-brand.

Chapter 3

1. Steve Jobs, "How to Live before You Die," Commencement Address, Stanford University, 2005.

2. Home Builders Federation, "Reversing the Decline of Small Housebuilders," 2017, https://www.hbf.co.uk/documents/6879/HBF_SME_Report_2017_Web.pdf.

3. IPPR, "Back Small Builders to Break the Stranglehold of Big Developers and Boost Housebuilding" (December 20, 2017), https://www.hbf.co.uk/documents/6879/HBF_SME_Report_2017_Web.pdf.

4. Marshall Lux and Robert Greene, "The State and Fate of Community Banking," M-RCBG Associate Working Paper no. 37, Mossavar-Rahmani Center for Business and Government, Kennedy School of Government, Harvard University, 2015, https://www.hks.harvard.edu/centers/mrcbg/publications/awp/awp37.

5. For more about the Massive Small Collective, see the website, mission statement, and information about forthcoming publications: https://www.massivesmall.org/.

6. US Chamber of Commerce Foundation, *Food Truck Nation*, 2018, https://www.foodtrucknation.us/wp-content/themes/food-truck-nation/Food-Truck-Nation-Full-Report.pdf.

Chapter 4

1. "London Property Prices," *Bloomberg*, 2019, https://www.bloomberg.com/graphics/property-prices/london/.

2. "Average Salary in London 2019," *Salary Explorer*, 2019, http://www.salaryexplorer.com/salary-survey.php?loc=3285&loctype=3.

3. "Housing for War," *Fortune* (October 1942), 95.

4. "Housing Crises Ahead, WPA Survey Finds," *Washington Post* (February 9, 1941), 13.

5. Holly Chamberlain, "Permanence in a Time of War: Three Defense Homes Corporation Projects in the Washington DC Metropolitan Area," in Richard Longstreth, ed., *Housing Washington: Two Centuries of Residential*

Development and Planning in the National Capitol Area (Washington, DC: Center for American Places, 2010).

6. National Housing Agency, "Zoning in Relation to the Homes Utilization Program," Division of Urban Studies, Bulletin No. 6 (October 8, 1942).

7. Arnold M. Rose, "Living Arrangements of the Urban Unattached," *American Journal of Sociology* 53, no. 6 (May 1948): 483–93.

8. Charles Abrams, "Billet the War Workers," *New Republic* (November 23, 1942), 673–74.

9. Frank Krutnik, "Critical Accommodations: Washington, Hollywood, and the World War II Housing Shortage," *Journal of American Culture* 30, no. 4 (2007): 417–33.

10. National Housing Agency, "Zoning."

11. Ibid.

12. Federal Home Loan Board, "Progress and Prospects in the War Housing Program, and War-Time Housing in Britain," in Federal Home Loan Bank Review, 1942.

13. Federal Works Agency, "Recent Migration into Washington, DC," Memo A3776, Works Progress Administration (January 5, 1942).

14. American Society of Planning Officials, "Conversions of Large Multiple-Family Dwellings to Single-Family Dwellings," Information Report No. 5, Planning Advisory Service (August 1949).

15. Paul Kelsey Williams, "Southwest Neighborhood, Razed 1960s," in *Lost Washington, DC* (London: Pavilion Books, 2012), 90–91.

16. "New Home-Building Brexit Slump: Construction of New Private Housing in London Falls to Lowest Level for Seven Years," *Homes & Property Newsletter* (August 8, 2019), https://www.homesandproperty.co.uk/property-news/new-homebuilding-brexit-slump-construction-of-new-private-housing-in-london-falls-to-lowest-level-a132606.html, updated in fall of 2019 with data from https://tradingeconomics.com/united-states/housing-starts.

17. Anna Minton, "The Great London Property Squeeze," *Guardian* (May 25, 2017), https://www.theguardian.com/society/2017/may/25/london-property-squeeze-affordable-housing.

18. Office for National Statistics, "Overcrowding and Under-occupation in England and Wales" (April 17, 2014), https://www.bl.uk/britishlibrary/~/media/bl/global/social-welfare/pdfs/non-secure/o/v/e/overcrowding-and-underoccupation-in-england-and-wales.pdf.

19. Annabel Dixon, citing Q&A about the British government's Rent-a-Room scheme (April 1, 2019), https://www.zoopla.co.uk/discover/renting/q-a-rent-a-room-scheme/#MSEiI2JRT8hQOjX0.97.

20. Office for National Statistics, "Households and Household Composition in England and Wales: 2001–11" (May 29, 2014).

21. MW Solicitors, "Affordable Housing" (July 27, 2016), https://mwsolicitors.co.uk/component/content/article?id=353:affordable-housing.

22. Skyler Olsen, *Doubled Up for Dollars*, Zillow Research (October 9, 2014), https://www.zillow.com/research/doubling-up-households-7947/.

23. Ibid.

24. Mireya Navarro, "Looser Rules on Illegal Housing Sought," *New York Times* (October 13, 2013), https://www.nytimes.com/2013/10/14/nyregion/looser-rules-on-illegal-housing-sought.html?.

25. Scott Adams, "How I (Almost) Saved the Earth," *Wall Street Journal* (August 21, 2010), https://www.wsj.com/articles/SB10001424052748704868604575433620189923744.

Chapter 5

1. Justin Moyer, "As 'Slacker' Turns 20, Director Linklater Reflects on the Film," *Washington Post*, Style Section (July 15, 2011), https://www.washingtonpost.com/lifestyle/style/as-slacker-turns-20-director-linklater-reflects-on-the-film/2011/07/07/gIQAzUxcGI_story.html?utm_term=.1cb8d1af0278.

2. Author interview with Richard Linklater, December 2017.

3. Dan Solomon, "The Church of the SubGenius Finally Plays It Straight," *Texas Monthly* (November 2, 2017), https://www.texasmonthly.com/the-daily-post/the-church-of-the-subgenius-finally-plays-it-straight/.

4. Farhad Mirza and Anna Calori, "Marc Ribot: Barriers to Participation," *Guernica* (April 3, 2017), https://www.guernicamag.com/marc-ribot-barriers-to-participation/. (CBGB was a New York music club, open 1973 to 2006, often considered the birthplace of punk.)

5. Robert M. Cyert and James G. March, *A Behavioral Theory of the Firm* (Upper Saddle River, NJ: Prentice Hall, 1963, 2d ed., 1992), 44.

6. Author interview with Richard Linklater, December 2017.

7. OECD, "New Forms of Work in the Digital Economy," Paris, 2016, 23, http://www.oecd.org/officialdocuments/publicdisplaydocumentpdf/?cote=DSTI/ICCP/IIS(2015)13/FINAL&docLanguage=En.

8. Upwork and Freelancers Union, "New Study Finds Freelance Economy Grew to 55 Million Americans This Year, 35% of Total U.S. Workforce," press release, 2016, https://www.upwork.com/press/2016/10/06/freelancing-in-america-2016/.

9. OECD Data, "Self-Employment Rate," 2018, https://data.oecd.org/emp/self-employment-rate.htm.

10. Megan Dunn, "Who Chooses Part-Time Work and Why?" *Monthly Labor Review* (March 2018), https://www.bls.gov/opub/mlr/2018/article/who-chooses-part-time-work-and-why.htm.

11. Deloitte, "Freelance Flexibility with Full-Time Stability," *Deloitte Millennial Survey 2017*, https://www2.deloitte.com/global/en/pages/about-deloitte/articles/millennial-survey-freelance-flexibility.html#opportunities.

12. Email interview with Charlotte Castle, November 27, 2017.

13. Samuel R. Delany, *Stars in My Pocket like Grains of Sand* (New York: Bantam Books, 1984), 115.

14. Linklater interview.

Chapter 6

1. Long Now Foundation, "The 10,000-Year Clock," http://longnow.org/clock/.

2. Eric Reynolds, "Creative Regenerator," *Spitalfields Life* (November 2, 2010), http://spitalfieldslife.com/2010/11/02/eric-reynolds-creative-regenerator/.

3. Ibid.

4. Ibid.

Chapter 7

1. Andy Gensler, "Underground Venues Seek Safety and Survival after Oakland Warehouse Fire," *Billboard* (December 9, 2016), https://www.billboard.com/articles/news/7616676/underground-venues-warehouse-fire-safety.

2. Erica Meltzer, "Denver Fire Describes Hazards at Rhinoceropolis: How Can Denver Keep Its DIY Arts Spaces?," *Denverite* (December 9, 2016), https://denverite.com/2016/12/09/denver-fire-describes-hazards-rhinoceropolis-not-permitted-residential-use/.

3. Jon Blistein, "Oakland Mayor Issues Order to Protect DIY Spaces after Ghost Ship Fire," *Rolling Stone* (January 12, 2017), https://www.rollingstone.com/music/music-news/oakland-mayor-issues-order-to-protect-diy-spaces-after-ghost-ship-fire-123732/.

4. Andrea Codrea-Rado, "Members of the DIY Community Compile Harm-Reduction Measures for Venues," *Vice* (December 6, 2016), https://www.vice.com/en_us/article/pg8m3b/oakland-fire-diy-community-harm.

5. Adriel Luis, "In the Aftermath of Oakland's Tragedy, How Museums Can Better Serve Local Arts and DIY Venues," *Smithsonian* (December 14, 2016), https://www.smithsonianmag.com/smithsonian-institution/aftermath-oaklands-tragedy-how-museums-can-better-serve-local-arts-and-diy-venues-180961418/.

6. Luke Broadwater, "Pugh Announces Task Force to Create 'Safe Art Spaces' in Baltimore after Foundry Evictions," *Baltimore Sun* (December 21, 2016), https://www.baltimoresun.com/maryland/baltimore-city/bs-md-ci-arts-spaces-20161221-story.html.

7. Leandro Medina and Friedrich Schneider, "Shadow Economies around the World: What Did We Learn Over the Last 20 Years?," IMF, WP/18/17 (January 2018), table 18.

8. Colin C. Williams, *Informal Sector Entrepreneurship*, Background Paper for the OECD Centre for Entrepreneurship, SMEs and Local Development, n.d., https://www.oecd.org/employment/leed/Background-Paper-PB-Informal-Entrepreneurship-final.pdf.

9. "Mayor Announces Shortlist for First-Ever Creative Enterprise Zones," Greater London Authority press release (March 20, 2018), https://www.london.gov.uk/press-releases/mayoral/mayor-announces-creative-enterprise-zone-shortlist; see also London Borough of Barking & Dagenham, *Our Growth Prospectus*, 2016, https://lbbd.gov.uk/our-growth-hubs.

10. *Naff*, British slang for "drab," "unfashionable," and "dull," is derived from "normal as fuck."

Chapter 8

1. This story can be found at Johnny Sanphillippo's blog, https://granolashotgun.com/2016/11/08/lessons-learned/.

2. Stewart Brand, in interview with Chris Anderson, TED Talk, April 2017, https://www.ted.com/talks/stewart_brand_and_chris_anderson_mammoths_resurrected_geoengineering_and_other_thoughts_from_a_futurist/transcript?language=en.

3. For more information, see https://leanurbanism.org/publications/the-story-of-lean-detroit/.

4. Position papers and case studies that were commissioned as part of this work can be found at www.leanurbanism.org. In addition, a book by J. P. Faber, *The New Pioneers*, tells stories from around the United States that influenced Lean Urbanism.

5. As they become available, all these tools and reports can be accessed at www.leanurbanism.org.

6. Author interview with Kevin Klinkenberg, September 6, 2019.

7. Ibid.

Chapter 9

1. UN Habitat, *Slum Almanac 2015–2016*, https://unhabitat.org/slum-almanac-2015-2016/.

2. HRH Charles, Prince of Wales, "A Speech by HRH The Prince of Wales at The Prince's Foundation for the Built Environment Conference 2009 Titled Globalization from the Bottom Up," 2009, https://www.princeofwales.gov.uk/speech/speech-hrh-prince-wales-princes-foundation-built-environment-conference-2009-titled.

3. UN Habitat, *Slum Almanac 2015–2016*.

4. Martha A. Chen, Sally Roever, and Caroline Skinner, "Urban Livelihoods: Reviewing the Evidence in Support of the New Urban Agenda," *Environment & Urbanization Brief* 34, IIED, 2016, 3, https://pubs.iied.org/pdfs/10808IIED.pdf.

5. Martha A. Chen, "The Urban Informal Economy: Towards More-Inclusive Cities," *Urbanet* (August 16, 2016), https://www.urbanet.info/urban-informal-economy/.

6. Quoted by Martha A. Chen, "Urban Employment in India: Trajectories and Trends," World Bank Workshop (New Delhi, June 7–8, 2011), ppt.

7. Eve Blau, "Revisiting Red Vienna as an Urban Project," 2016, http://www.austrianinformation.org/fall-2016/re-visiting-red-vienna-as-an-urban-project.

8. Ryan Holeywell, "Vienna Offers Affordable and Luxurious Housing," *Governing* (February 2013), https://www.governing.com/topics/health-human-services/gov-affordable-luxurious-housing-in-vienna.html.

9. James C. Scott, *Two Cheers for Anarchism: Six Easy Pieces on Autonomy, Dignity, and Meaningful Work and Play*, 2d ed. (Princeton, NJ: Princeton University Press, 2014), 12.

10. Stewart Brand, in interview with Chris Anderson, TED Talk, April 2017, as transcribed by Singju Post (February 1, 2018), https://singjupost.com/mammoths-resurrected-and-other-thoughts-from-a-futurist-stewart-brand-transcript/.

About the Author

Photo by Charles Seton

Hank Dittmar (1956–2018) is the author of *Transport and Neighbourhoods* (Edge Futures, 2008), *New Transit Town* (Island Press, 2004), and *My Kind of City* (Island Press, 2019). He is coauthor of *Sustainable Planet* (Beacon Press, 2000) and *Green Living* (Compendium, 2009). Before his death in 2018, he was a frequent contributor to *Building Design* magazine and also wrote for the *London Evening Standard*, the *Los Angeles Times*, the *Guardian*, the *New York Times*, and the *Washington Post*.

Dittmar was the founding principal of Hank Dittmar Associates, an international urban planning firm (2013–2018). Before that, he was chief executive of The Prince's Foundation for Building Community for nearly a decade, and prior to that was founding president and CEO of Reconnecting America, a national nonprofit that integrates transportation and community development. His long and varied career included service as a regional planner, airport director, policy advisor, and outreach worker with street gangs in Chicago. He was a visiting fellow at Kellogg College at Oxford University, Outstanding Alumnus of the Graduate School at the University of Texas at Austin, and winner of the Seaside Prize for his contributions to urban design worldwide.